# CONFIDENT
# INVESTING
## WHY BLIND TRUST IS A POOR STRATEGY

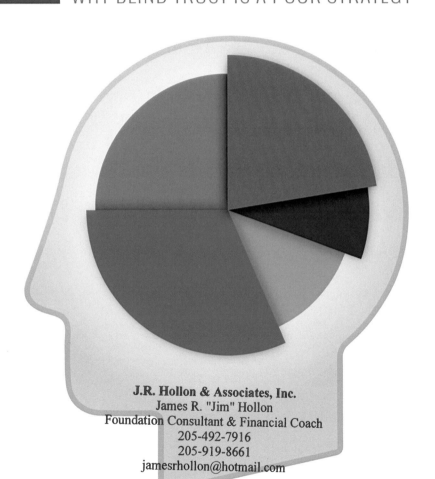

J.R. Hollon & Associates, Inc.
James R. "Jim" Hollon
Foundation Consultant & Financial Coach
205-492-7916
205-919-8661
jamesrhollon@hotmail.com

# PAUL WINKLER

For information or to order, please contact:
Paul Winkler, Inc.
3050 Business Park Circle Suite 503
Goodlettsville, TN 37072
615.851.1950
615.851.4597 (fax)

www.paulwinkler.net

Second Edition

**The Library of Congress Cataloging-in-Publication Data**

Winkler, Paul, author
Confident Investing / by Paul Winkler
Nashville, TN : Paul Winkler, Inc. 2018. | "Previously published in 2009."
Includes bibliographical references and index
Library of Congress Control Number: 2018913527
ISBN 978-0-578-44936-4 (hardcover)
ISBN 978-0-692-14789-4 (paper)
ISBN 978-0-692-14790-0 (Kindle)

1. Finance 2. Business 3. Self Help 4. Education
LC record available at https://lccn.loc.gov/2018913527

# Disclaimer:

As with all investment information, past performance is no guarantee of future results. There is no way to predict all the future variables that can affect stock and bond market returns. It is my intent that this book be used as a tool to help make the reader a better educated and savvier consumer of investment products and services. The information provided is general in nature and is provided for educational purposes only. It shall not be considered to be a solicitation for the sale of securities or investment products. Every investor's situation is different. This information is not intended to be a replacement for a qualified financial advisor.

—Paul Winkler, The Investor Coach

# Acknowledgments

I have so many to thank for their contributions to making this latest work possible. Writing a book that deals with a topic that is so important to so many people is a great responsibility. There is always the reality that something important will be left out and someone will find a typo someplace. In the writing of this work, I have been able to use some of the same material from my first book "Above the Maddening Crowd" and build on its foundation. As with the first work, many people are credited with helping me get this project off the ground - some of the same people and some new faces. I can only hope that I don't leave any out:

**My Wife Debbie**—As always, you have been the wind beneath my wings. Always believing in me and encouraging me to venture forth into new territory. I can't over-stress how important your love and support have been. You're the best.

**Mom and Dad**—I miss you both more each day. I have come to realize how lucky I have been to have the upbringing that I did. You taught me how to be the best I could be in anything I pursued. There was always a belief that all things were possible if we would just apply ourselves and pursue excellence. I simply can't thank you enough.

**My Whole Crew**—Jonathan, Jim, Evan, Ira, Dan, Arlene, Anne, Chad and the "newer" kids on the block: Chris and Michael who worked so hard "behind the scenes" to make this book a reality.

**Mark Matson**—Much of this book is a result of the coaching and teaching you've done over the years. I have gained so much wisdom and insight just by observing you in action and want to thank you for the consistent inspiration.

**My Sons Andrew and Alex**—You guys are still the absolute joy of my life. I love you and your mom more than you know. You both have grown to be stellar individuals and I couldn't be more proud.

**My Sisters Andrea and Debbie**—I still love hanging out with you guys and feel so fortunate to be part of your lives. Although we all live in different parts of the country, I think we are closer than ever.

**Our Clients**—I thank you all so much for the belief that you've shown in me and our company. Your willingness and desire to learn is what makes all of this possible. It was just a dream nearly two decades ago that we could build a company where education and application of academic principles of investing would be the foundation. Thanks for making it a reality.

**Jere Mitchum, Ph.D.**—Your book editing skills were a Godsend. Thanks so much for all of your effort and attention to detail.

**And finally to all my friends and fellow church members**—Your love and support have brought me great joy.

# Table of Contents

# Introduction

My introduction into the financial arena was characterized by a marked lack of anything truly relevant to wise investing. Like countless others in the financial services industry, I entered the world of finance through mutual fund and insurance sales. I will never forget the first time I walked into an insurance company sales office in upstate New York. I had just graduated from college with a degree in economics and a minor in business and felt that my education qualified me for whatever leadership role they might have available. I confidently approached the front desk and told the staff that I was looking for a job in management. My hopes were quickly dashed when the secretary explained that I would have to become a successful salesperson first, and then I might be able to move on to management. *A salesperson first? They never tell you that in school.*

Desperate for my first real job, I agreed to speak to the branch manager about a position in sales. The first interview was cordial enough, as the manager explained how the financial industry worked. He spoke at length about the huge income I could make selling insurance and investment products; quite frankly, the thought of making five times my current salary at my computer repair job was all I needed to take the next step.

Before I could continue the interview process, I had to take a test to see how well suited I was for the position. I arrived at the office early on test day and sat down in a small cubicle to take the test. To my surprise, the exam was filled with questions that seemed to have nothing to do with being a competent financial planner. The questions primarily revolved around how I dealt with rejection and whether I was outgoing or introverted. One question asked how I acted when entering a room of strangers. Did I retreat to a corner and keep to myself, or did I introduce myself to everyone?

It didn't take long to figure out how to play the test. I knew I had to answer every question in a way that showed I wasn't afraid of people. I understood that a career in selling probably meant a life of hearing 'no' more often than 'yes,' and I knew that they were looking for people who wouldn't take rejection personally. Sure enough, when my test results came in, I got a call from an ecstatic sales manager. He told me my test scores were through the roof, and he wanted me to come in as soon as possible for the second interview.

Needless to say, I was hired.

The next step was to pass all of the state exams for the insurance licenses I needed to hold in order to sell the company's products. By the time my first year under new employment came and went, I had passed the state insurance exams to sell life, health, disability, and property and casualty (home and auto) insurance, as well as the exams required to offer mutual funds and variable annuities.

My first year on the job was challenging in many ways. The classes I was required to take primarily focused on how the company's products worked and how to prospect for new business. Every once in a while, someone taught me a useful financial planning technique, but those moments were few and far between. Essentially, the name of the game was "smile and dial." Most of the advice I received from experienced advisors revolved more around prospecting and sales strategies than anything else, and the only advice I ever received about investment portfolio management ended up being completely wrong.

On top of being improperly trained, there was another obstacle in my way— my age. At twenty-five, I found it difficult to get people twice my age to take me seriously. That made the sales process all the more difficult. What could I possibly know that will help them plan their financial futures? My clients were probably thinking that—and I was, too. The problem was that I didn't have the right education to properly guide my potential clients through the financial maze.

I decided that I needed a few designations behind my name before I would be taken seriously. After achieving the first designation, I noticed something that surprised me. The process of gaining clients' trust and hence their business became no easier. The reaction I was hoping for—something like, "You're a Life Underwriter Training Council Fellow®? My wife and I have got to work with you"—didn't exactly come. The answer, I thought once again, was to get more designations. I became a Chartered Life Underwriter®, a Chartered Financial Consultant®, a Registered Financial Consultant®, and so on, ad nauseam. While I learned a great deal, my goal of instant credibility was never attained. I was still just a salesperson in the investment and financial planning industry.

Then I thought perhaps the solution was to change broker/dealers. (A broker/dealer is a company that is registered with the Securities and Exchange Commission and is allowed to sell securities to the public or for itself.) I attended broker/dealer conventions looking for answers, and I wandered up and down the aisles listening to all the wholesalers' sales pitches as they feverishly presented their products to salespeople like me. It was an overload of information (but I did get some nice pens and stress balls for all my efforts).

I struggled with many of the concepts that the wholesalers taught at their booths. In my mind, the numbers didn't add up. They used overly optimistic numbers to make their financial products stand out. They always seemed to focus our attention on the mutual funds they managed that had just had stellar performance; yet they virtually ignored the poor performers in their inventory.

Other elements of the industry didn't make sense to me either. For example, there were numerous companies who offered to help manage their clients' portfolios on a fee basis, but their methods of fund management never seemed right. One company in particular puzzled me. They said they would carefully watch the various funds in the portfolio, which they probably did. But when they changed the mix between different asset categories (like from large to small U.S. stocks), the company's fund managers would automatically buy or sell the changed category in another part of the portfolio to make up the difference. To me, that was like hiring a maid to clean your house, and then following behind her throwing things on the floor.

The head of one of the broker/dealers caught my attention one day during a lecture on tax and financial planning. He was one of the most successful men I had ever met (income-wise), so I thought it might be a good idea to listen to him. I listened with great interest as he explained the process of putting together someone's financial picture. The idea was to sell the client an oil and gas limited partnership for the intangible drilling cost deductions (8 percent commission), as well as a low income housing REIT for the tax credits available (8 percent commission), and then combine that with other REITs that kicked off income (another 7 percent commission). The tax deductions or credits could offset the income from the taxable investments. Next, take the cash flow from the limited partnership and buy a variable universal life policy (90 percent commission), borrow the cash value, invest in outside mutual funds (5.75 percent commission), and deduct the interest . . . and on and on. His goal, as he put it, was to confuse the client to the point that they became putty in his hands and bought whatever he recommended.

I questioned this powerful man's tactics and advice at length with an advisor at breakfast, and it was there that the advisor gave me one of the best pieces of advice I had ever received. He recommended that I invest some money in my own education by pursuing investment studies outside the financial product sales side of the industry. He assured me that I would never hear any objective information about investing until I removed myself from the mutual fund and insurance companies who stood to gain if I sold their products. It made perfect sense after several years of nothing making sense—and that advice started me on a journey that continues to this day.

What follows is the culmination of years of study as well as research from academics from such places as the University of Chicago, Yale University, MIT, and Harvard, to name a few. My goal is to make this information understandable to each and every investor, regardless of his or her level of knowledge in investing. I often joke with my clients that I believe my mother passed through Missouri when she was pregnant with me. That's the only way I can explain my desire to have to know why something works rather than just know it works. You have to "show me" or I won't be convinced. In that spirit, I use results from numerous academic studies to explain the philosophies taught in this book.

Call me crazy, but I believe investing should make sense.

There are over 280,000 financial advisors in the U.S., over 385,000 insurance sales agents, the thousands of insurance and brokerage firms they work for, twenty-four- hour a day media streaming from every direction, and countless other do-it- yourselfers and self-titled "experts" who are more than willing to dispense advice on what they think the market is doing.[1] Everybody wants to tell you how to beat the market and find the next best deal or the best undervalued stocks. The media in all its forms is ready with the tips, tricks, and timing that could make you the next millionaire. It really does seem like a circus, a cacophony of sounds and smoke and mirrors.

But there is a way to escape the marketing madness —and that's where educated investors can be. Knowledge and education are powerful forces, and this could be no truer anywhere than in the world of investing. For beginner and expert investors alike, I hope to shed some light on the complex realm of investing through teaching basic principles, dispelling common investment myths, and providing real-world solutions for managing your money.

Wall Street and the media would have us believing that there are short cuts and tricks of the trade to make big money, and to make it fast. In the following pages, I'll show you there is no hocus pocus or magic to investing. Instead, we'll discuss researched ideas, as I provide practical tools that you can actually use. There is a way to invest that won't make you nervous every single time the market moves. And you don't have to lose sleep worrying about your retirement. We'll drown out the investment noise as we reveal what history has shown to be a better, sounder, and more proven way to invest.

It has been quite a ride since the first time I walked through the doors at that financial office in upstate New York. I hope that my experiences will be your gain as you discover the hidden world of investing and the truths behind the Wall Street Marketing Machine.

## CHAPTER ONE

# THE INVESTOR'S DILEMMA

# The Investor's Dilemma

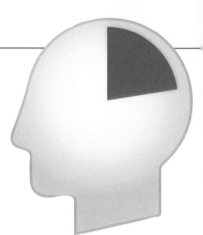

**W**hy do investors fail? This is a question that has plagued me for years. On the surface, it seems that investors should be a happy and prosperous lot. The return figures reported by mutual fund companies are almost always in the double-digit range. Who would complain about that? Yet investors become easily disillusioned when it comes to the stock market—and for good reason. According to Dalbar Research in Boston, the average equity investor earned a trivial 3.98 percent return from 1987 to 2016, while large U.S. stocks, as measured by the S&P 500, averaged over ten percent during the same time period. Why then do investors often get such poor results, when the double-digit figures reported by the market at large would seem to indicate that the situation should be otherwise?

The answer lies in a perpetual cycle that investors go through when it comes to making investment decisions. It is a cycle that is often incredibly beneficial to the investment industry in general, but it can be highly detrimental to the individual investor. That cycle is called "The Investor's Dilemma."

## What is the Investor's Dilemma?

The Investor's Dilemma is a seven-phase cycle that people go through which ultimately ends in frustration with the investing process. Some of the steps are psychological in nature, while others are related to the actions we take based on "stinking thinking". Even though we all desire a positive outcome regarding our investment experiences, it is this cycle that often prevents the success we so desperately need in order to maintain our standard of living in retirement.

## Step One: Fear of the Future

The Investor's Dilemma begins with a fear of the future. Fear is nothing unusual— and it is certainly nothing new. We all have fears and misgivings when it comes to money. Yearly, monthly, weekly, and even daily, we find ourselves concerned with the possibility of market declines that erode investment values, the chance of missing out on big market upsides, the apprehension of paying too much for investment advice and finding out that it was lousy advice, and the likelihood of getting lower returns than we should have gotten. Ultimately, it all boils down to one underlying fear: *People are afraid they will run out of money before they run out of life.*

These fears intensify as retirement nears, because it causes us to reevaluate our previous investment decisions and face the reality that we must make better investment decisions or be faced with working many more years than we initially intended. When we're younger, it is easy to feel bulletproof—we're invincible and relatively unconcerned about the future. After all, we have plenty of time ahead of us to build our investments and save. The thinking is, "If I make a mistake, there is always time to rectify it." With age, though, comes the realization that time is a precious commodity.

## Step Two: Prediction of the Future

Since we have this inherent fear of the future, it is only natural that we would desire a prediction of future market events as it relates to our money and investments. We subconsciously wish that someone could tell us—with great certainty—what is likely to happen down the road. We want the answers to questions like: *Where will U.S. markets go? What's going to happen overseas? What is ahead for the economy at large? Who are going to be the great fund managers? Who seems to have a handle on this thing called the "market?"* If we could find the answers to these questions, then we would feel safe, knowing that the future was in good hands; and we, the individual investors, would know our money was secure.

The investment and financial industry is aware of our intrinsic desire to know what lies ahead. They also know that, instinctively, we want to survive, so they will go to great lengths to make us feel like we're getting both the best information and the best investments available. The question then becomes how can the experts—or anyone for that matter—predict the future?

Well, if you were trying to figure out who is going to succeed in college, where would you look? Logically, you would be inclined to look at students who did well in high school. It just makes sense. If you want to figure out who is going to be a star quarterback this year, you would naturally look at who did well last year. This same idea directly applies to predictions about investments. In short, if you want to find out what funds or stocks are likely to do well in the future, you are, understandably, first going to look at what did well in the past.

## Step Three: Past Performance

Pick up the latest copy of any financial magazine, and chances are high that you will see dozens of references to past performance showered all over the covers and within the pages. You'll likely see article titles such as *Ten Five-Star Fund Managers, Five Funds You Can Count On,* and *Six Stocks for the Year Ahead.* Even the advertisements make references to funds' Morningstar™ ratings. Morningstar™ gives Five Stars for those funds in the top ten percent of their peer group and Four Stars for the next 22.5 percent, and fund manager and investment companies will use these ratings in their ads. The message is clear—the industry wants you to think you can put your trust in the fund managers and investment gurus who have gotten the job done in the past.

*Does it work?* If we're talking about getting investors to buy a fund, you bet it does. According to the Wall Street Journal, "funds that earned high star ratings attracted the vast majority of investor dollars." In fact, according to Morningstar, in 2016 four and five star funds garnered $303 billion in inflows compared to $98 billion in inflows to one and two star funds.[2] Clearly, these ratings—which are all based on past performance—attract a lot of attention from the average person looking for a shortcut to making investing decisions.

More importantly, though, does it work for individual investors like us? The answer to that question is a resounding "NO." Focusing on the past encourages investors to concentrate on yesterday's winners, but that is just like driving down the road with your eyes in the rear-view mirror.

So why does the industry do it? Ultimately, it boils down to pure marketing. Investment companies, firms, and portfolio managers want to sell more mutual funds; they know that using past performance figures will attract the majority of the new money being invested, so they use those numbers. It's that simple. Investors think past performance is helpful, so the industry will use that data to sell investments. This is evidenced by the articles in trade magazines, the talking heads on TV, and the sales pitches of investment advisors all around the country.

## Step Four: Information Overload

We live in one of the most amazing periods in history, with access to amounts of information that is virtually unprecedented. The Internet has revolutionized most of our business practices—but it is not without its complications. As human beings, hard wired to process information in a certain methodical way, we aren't capable of properly processing all of the data being thrown at us on a daily basis; thus, we are literally drowning in information. It was the great promise that, with the advent of the personal computer and subsequently, the World Wide Web, we would have access to unlimited amounts of information that would surely make our lives easier. *What happened?* Now we have so much information that it is almost paralyzing.

I refer to this modern state of information overload as the Harry Nilsson Syndrome. Remember the lyrics of his old song "Everybody's talkin' at me, but I don't hear a word they're sayin'?" Simply put, it's mass confusion at every turn. One publication says that X, Y, and Z are the best funds. Another magazine has a completely different list of the "must have" funds. The expert broker on TV says they're both wrong. In fact, just try to Google the word "investments," and you'll get over 246 million hits on your computer. There are stock tips galore, investor alerts running rampant, and every kind of advice under the sun on what you should do with your hard earned money.

Like Southwest Airlines says, "Wanna Get Away?"

## Step Five: Emotion or Instinct-Based Decisions

As humans, we are continually driven by our instincts and emotions. When we're overloaded with information, our emotions and feelings go into overdrive; and that's when we tend to make bad decisions. This is yet another point that the investment industry—and virtually every other industry—uses against us. In fact, using this detail against us is ingrained in many salespeople as a commonly used sales tactic. There is a universal truth in the sales world that people buy on emotion and justify with logic, and salespeople use this to their advantage by learning how to appeal to the emotions instead of calling on reason and intellect.

***Fear.*** Humans have a handful of strong emotions that often fall prey to salespeople's tactics. One of these emotions is fear. People often think, "I have no idea what to do. I guess I'll just stick my money under the mattress." Maybe they just put all their money into a CD or a guaranteed annuity, believing that it will be safe there. The fear of making a colossal mistake and losing some or all of their money leads them to this general attitude, "It is better to do nothing or search out guarantees at all costs than to throw my money away on a bad investment decision."

***Greed.*** Another strong emotion is greed. Unlike their fearful counterparts, a person driven by greed can become overly confident. "I've got this. Investing is easy." They throw caution to the wind, trying every scheme that seems to hold the promise of making them rich quickly.

***Loyalty and Trust.*** These two emotions often drive our decision-making as well. When we don't know what to do or who to believe—especially in light of how many out there claim to be "experts"—we can be easily influenced by a family member, an old family friend, or fall back onto familiar investments. We find ourselves justifying our investment decisions by saying

- "My dad worked at that company all of his life."
- "My husband loved that company's products."
- "I don't know. I just like that guy."
- "That magazine has a pretty logo."

And on the list goes. When friends and family are involved, it is easy to be swayed by their investment decisions with no thought to the fact that they may have a far more aggressive strategy than you, or that they have been given bad advice themselves.

Emotions play a clear and important role in our decision-making process, but instincts are just as significant. We are inherently driven away from pain and gravitate toward pleasure. We abhor pain—any kind of pain. It is painful to invest in mutual funds that haven't performed well in the past three to five years. It's like betting on a horse that just lost its last five races. Our brains have difficulty processing that kind of thinking. We think, *surely it will lose the next one as well.* Similarly we are driven to buy the funds with strong track records. *This fund has averaged fifteen percent since its inception. It must be a good one.*

## Step Six: Breaking the Rules

When reason and rational decision-making is replaced by emotion, following the rules is generally not a primary concern. Consequently, when we invest with our emotions it won't be long before we break the rules of investing. What are these rules? Without even realizing it, you've probably heard them a hundred times. ***In fact, the investment industry has pounded them into our brains; which is ironic, because it is typically the industry players who most often break the very rules they advocate.***

One widespread rule is **Buy Low, Sell High.** This seems obvious, but in reality, it's actually quite hard to do. It is analogous to losing weight. Diet and nutrition experts tell us that all we have to do is "eat less and move more." It sounds simple enough, yet it is often seemingly impossible to carry out. The main reason that the *Buy Low, Sell High* rule is so hard to abide by is that markets and stock prices run in unpredictable cycles.

When friends see me in public, they will often ask, "Hey Paul, what's the market going to do?"

My reply is always the same. "It will go up, then down, up, then down… and not necessarily in that order."

We laugh and then go about our business. Yes, we laugh, but the funny thing is, I'm not kidding. If we buy a fund that has had recent stellar performance, where is it in the cycle? It is up! You can probably guess what follows up. All of the highest returning funds in 1999 had a healthy dose of tech stocks as investments. We all know where that led—down, down, and then down. By focusing us on past performance, as we are encouraged to do, the investment world often causes us to buy high. It is no wonder that we don't get the desired results we seek. Rarely is anything so cut and dry as the rule of Buy Low, Sell High.

Another rule of investing is to **Diversify.** As the saying goes, *don't put all of your eggs in one basket.* The trouble is that when we buy funds based on past performance, we are often getting into funds that contain all of the stocks that have gone up in the past few years. When we do a little research, we often find that our mutual funds often contain many of the same stocks because it is based on performance rather than diversity. In this case, the investor is experiencing what I call "perceived diversification." The stocks may have all been good performers, but no one has taken care to ensure that the stocks span multiple asset classes, which can help safeguard a portfolio against a particular market segment downturn.

Many of us have heard the warning: **Don't try to time the market. You can't possibly figure out the market's future direction.** I agree wholeheartedly with this statement. Time and time again, studies show that investors who try to predict the market's direction will get burned. As common knowledge as this fact may be, it is not unusual to find investment managers doing just that. Of course, they don't call it "market timing," but that is exactly what they are attempting to do—play with market timing. It may come in the form of holding large amounts of cash in the fund or waiting for the right "opportunity." The fund manager may also drift into segments of the market in the hope that they've miraculously spotted a trend in the making.

We've also heard that it is wise to **Buy and Hold.** *Once you've invested, it is best to sit tight. And whatever you do, don't try to day-trade.* Yes, that's what we hear from the mutual fund companies and their sales forces, but what is really happening behind the scenes? According to Investopedia, the average "managed stock" fund turnover rate is approximately 130%. That means that they are completely changing what stocks are held in the fund on an annual basis. So, while we the individual investors are buying and *holding*, fund managers are moving our money all over the place.

So why do the "experts" engage in these practices? There are two probable motives. The first is fairly innocent—some fund managers truly believe that they can beat the market. In a TV show I saw several years ago, John Stossel interviewed Princeton professor Burton Malkiel about this issue. Malkiel said it was like "giving up a belief in Santa Claus." I think it's more like giving up a belief in *yourself*. Imagine being a highly educated fund manager. You've studied the stock market for years, and you've studied with the best and brightest in the investment field. Now you're told that you must accept that you have no ability to choose stocks that will do better than the market does all on its own. It is a humbling thought and not an easy pill to swallow for veteran investment gurus.

The other reason is a little less innocent—and it has to do with marketing. Since the majority of money flows to funds with the best short-term performance (and for the record, ten years is short-term in the world of stocks), a fund manager is forced to gamble with the portfolio. It is one of the only ways to have top-shelf performance. In other words, if I want my fund to be in the top-ranked funds—the ones that get all the press—I have to trade stocks and get in and out of the market in hopes of hitting a quick home run without taking a hit. Since most investors are unaware that the success is random, the risk is worth taking if it results in money flowing toward the fund they are managing.

## Step Seven: Performance Losses

The final step of the Investor's Dilemma is performance losses. Performance losses come in three varieties. The first type is called a *capital loss*. When we hear stories about investors who lost everything, it was the result of a capital loss. This type of loss is when you invest in an individual stock and the company goes bankrupt. Examples from the news include Toys "R" Us, Radio Shack, Eastman Kodak, General Motors, Chrysler, and Lehman Brothers.

The second type of loss is a *market loss*. Market losses don't just affect certain companies; they affect most companies in a certain area of the market. For example, when the technology bubble burst, nearly all the companies in that area of the market tumbled in value, and investors lost money whether they owned two or two hundred tech stocks.

The final type of loss often goes completely undetected by investors. It is referred to as a *relative loss*. A relative loss can be difficult for average investors to identify because they may not necessarily be losing money. This type of loss is the result of a fund or other investment vehicle that you own delivering returns that are less than the area of the market in which you are investing. For instance, if you are in a large company stock fund and it underperforms the Standard and Poor's 500 (the large company stock index more commonly known as the S&P 500), then you have suffered a relative loss. If and when these losses are discovered, investors usually find themselves back at the beginning of the Investor's Dilemma—fear of the future. And so the dilemma continues.

## Escaping the Investor's Dilemma

In all of my years spent working with investors, I've only found one tried and true way to help investors escape the frustrating cycle of the Investor's Dilemma.

The solution is education.

I strongly believe that most investors don't want to know every last detail about investing, but they do want a basic foundation in investments and a general knowledge of the market and key terminology. They want to understand enough so they feel confident that they are doing the right things with their money. Confident investors—or in other words, those who are educated—have peace of mind regarding their investment decisions. They don't worry about every slight change in the economy or what the Chairman of the Federal Reserve is going to announce next week, and they're not concerned with every movement of the market. They can leave these concerns behind, because they know four crucial things. Educated investors know

1. What they are doing.

2. Why they are doing it.

3. What their costs are.

4. What to expect.

Throughout this book I will provide the information that will help you become a confident investor. My goal is to provide information to you in an entertaining and stimulating way. Since most people are visual learners, I will be using multiple visual aids to help you "see" how investing works. Because investing is also largely concerned with numbers, I will be using some light mathematics for example purposes. Don't worry—it won't get too complicated.

I will begin by describing some of the basic components of investing. We'll cover fundamental topics such as *What is a stock? What is a bond?* For those of you who've been investing for a while, it will be a nice refresher course of the basics. It's always good to get back to essentials. I will then move to the more advanced aspects of investing. Investing doesn't have to be complicated—in fact, everyone can and *should* understand the basic principles. It is critical for peace of mind.

Some say that knowledge is power; it's really *applied knowledge* that holds the key to your financial success. So use the following pages as a road-map to understand and take control of your financial future. For it is not simply the facts and figures in these pages that will lead you to becoming a successful investor. Rather, it is your practical application of them in the real world.

## Summary

- The question that plagues the financial world is why do investors fail? The answer lies in a perpetual cycle called the Investor's Dilemma.

- The Investor's Dilemma is a seven-phase cycle that ultimately ends in frustration with the investing process. There are seven phases or steps in the Investor's Dilemma.

- <u>Step One:</u> Fear of the Future. Ultimately, it all boils down to one underlying fear: People are afraid they will run out of money before they run out of life.

- <u>Step Two:</u> Prediction of the Future. We feel that if we could just know where the market is heading, we would feel safe, knowing that the future was in good hands.

- <u>Step Three:</u> Past Performance. Using past performance as an indicator for individual investors simply does not work.

- <u>Step Four:</u> Information Overload. The amount of information available to us today is almost paralyzing in its volume. Investors must be selective as to what they pay attention to.

- <u>Step Five:</u> Emotion or Instinct-Based Decisions. As humans, we are continually driven by our instincts and emotions. The most common emotions that drive our decisions are: fear, greed, loyalty and trust.

- <u>Step Six:</u> Breaking the Rules. When reason and rational decision-making is replaced by emotion, following the rules is generally not a primary concern. The most common rules of investing are: 1) Buy low, sell high 2) Diversify 3) Don't try to time the market 4) Buy and hold.

- <u>Step Seven:</u> Performance Losses. Performance losses come in three varieties. The first type is called a capital loss. The second type of loss is a market loss. The final type of loss is a relative loss.

- The only real and lasting solution to escape the Investor's Dilemma is education.

- Educated investors know what they are doing, why they are doing it, what their costs are, and what to expect.

## Quick Quiz

1. Why do investors fail?

2. What is the Investor's Dilemma?

3. What are the seven steps of the Investor's Dilemma?

4. What is most investors' biggest underlying fear?

5. With age comes the realization that time is a _____ _____.

6. When investors are trying to determine where to invest their money, what is typically the first (and fatal) mistake they inherently make?

7. Why does the investment industry put such an emphasis on past performance?

8. What fact about humans do salespeople utilize as a sales tactic?

9. When we don't know what to do or who to believe, what or who are we easily influenced by?

10. One common rule of investing is don't put all your eggs in one basket. What is the technical term for this phrase?

11. What is the most common outcome of engaging in market timing?

12. What two motivating factors drive investors to engage in unwise investment practices such as market timing?

13. How do we escape the investor's dilemma?

14. Some say that knowledge is power; it's really _____ _____ that holds the key to your financial success.

An investment in knowledge
always pays the best
interest.

Benjamin Franklin

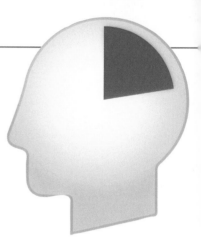

# Understanding Bonds

**I**t is said that the great Vince Lombardi, legendary coach for the Green Bay Packers, started every season with a team meeting. Coach Lombardi would hold a football high in the air proclaiming to rookies and veterans alike, "Gentleman, this is a football." In his own unique way, Lombardi was saying that the key to greatness is to be brilliant at the basics, never forgetting where it all begins.

Since this is primarily a book about investing, it seems appropriate to start off by developing an understanding of some of the primary building blocks of an investment portfolio. Too often, we jump into complex topics, but lack an understanding of the foundation. The result is that we tend to draw faulty conclusions and end up making grave mistakes that could cost us our financial futures.

## Give Me Money

Some say that it takes money to make money—and for the corporate world, truer words were never spoken. Equipment, infrastructure, distribution, advertising, and every other aspect of business all require money before a single light switch can be flipped. Raising several billion dollars for a company's operations is often no easy task—it's not as simple as going down to the local bank for a loan. Because of this, corporations turn to the public markets for capital, and one way they raise money in this market is through the issuance of bonds.

## What is a Bond?

A *bond* is simply a tool that is used when a company, mortgagee, or governmental unit borrows money. Bonds are usually issued in even denominations of $1,000, $5,000 and $10,000, and they typically have a certain period of time before they *mature* (or end). For instance, if an investor buys a $1,000 ten-year bond, he can expect to receive the bond's face value (or $1,000) back ten years from the date the money was first borrowed. During this ten-year period, the borrower makes interest payments to the lender/investor.

In the old days, bonds had coupons attached to them for the interest payments, which were redeemed on a regular basis by the lender/investor. Because of our increasingly paperless way of doing business, this method of paying interest is no longer used, but the term coupon is still used to refer to the interest payment associated with the bond. Most bonds make interest payments every six months, or semi-annually.

## Why Invest in Bonds?

Author Mark Twain once said, "I am more concerned about the return *of* my money than the return *on* my money." My guess is that Mr. Twain was a bond investor, because one of the main reasons we invest in bonds is because of their stability. Many bondholders choose bonds for this very reason, and consequently, they are among the first groups in line to get their money back when the issuer of their bonds runs into financial difficulty. As we'll see later, though, bonds often go up in value when stocks go down. This reduces volatility when stock markets aren't doing well. Unfortunately, many investors get impatient with the lower returns that they usually see associated with bonds and break this cardinal rule.

One type of bond is a *high-yield bond*. By definition, high-yield bonds are those issued by companies in financial distress. When the market goes down and the economy falters, it is these distressed companies that often default on their loans. This can cause both the stock and bond segments of our investments to go down together. This occurred in the stock and high-yield bond market during the economic downturn in late 2007, 2008 and early 2009. Many high-yield bond funds lost 40% or more of their value at the same time stocks declined in value. The mistake that investors often make is that they invest in these so-called high-yield bonds to increase their returns, but anytime we have the potential for greater returns, as is the case with high-yield bonds, we must realize that there is greater risk involved.

## Maturity Ranges

There are three typical maturity ranges associated with bonds:

1. ***Short-Term***—Less than five years.

2. ***Intermediate***—Between five and ten years.

3. ***Long-Term***—Over ten years.

The greater the amount of time a bond has until it matures, the greater the potential amount of volatility that can be experienced by the investor. The major cause of fluctuations in bonds is *interest rate risk*.

## Interest Rate Risk

I fondly remember one of my favorite childhood activities on the elementary school playground was riding the seesaw. The concept of a seesaw is simple enough; If you find someone nearly equal in weight, each time you push off the ground and go up, your friend will go down—and vice versa. Investing in bonds can be a lot like that old childhood toy. When interest rates climb, bonds prices go down. When interest rates drop, bond prices increase. To understand why this occurs, let's look at a simple example.

Let's say that I've decided to buy a single bond issued by a well-established corporation. This bond matures in five years, has a triple-A rating (more on ratings below), and has a six percent coupon (interest) rate. In year one of our example, I invest the $1,000. For the next five years, I would expect to receive $60 (which is six percent of $1,000) per year, or $30 every six months. Visually, it would look like this:

## ABC Corporation 5-Year Bond

Now imagine that one year from the date I made my $1,000 investment, interest rates climbed such that new bonds were paying more to investors than they were just a year ago. For example, let's say our corporation would now have to pay eight percent on the new four-year bonds they are issuing. (Note that this four-year bond will mature at the same time that my five-year bond will mature, because it was issued in year two of my five-year bond.)

Now here is the question, if I want to sell my five-year bond, what must I do to entice someone to buy it from me? The problem I face is that my bond will still only pay $60 per year for the remaining four years, and the new $1,000 bonds are paying $80 per year. The only way to sell my bond is to drop the price. In other words, I must discount the bond so that the investor choosing between my bond and the new, four-year bond will be indifferent between the two alternatives. Investors must get the same yield or return regardless of which bond they choose to buy. Again, visually, it would look like this:

## ABC Corporation 5-Year Bond

## ABC Corporation 4-Year Bond

The investor in the six percent bond will be just as happy receiving $60 per year because he paid only $934 for the bond, and he will of course receive $1,000 when the bond matures. Thus, it is easy to see how risk rises as a bond's years to maturity increase. The longer an investor holds on to old, lower yielding bonds, the longer he must accept lower interest, and demand greater discounts.

## Risks of Bond Investing

**Credit Risk.** Go down to your local check-cashing location and you will find many people who are credit risks walking in and out of the doors. Check cashing businesses charge high rates for their services, but when people have poor credit that may be their only option, and they usually have to pay more to borrow money. The same is true in the world of capital.

The lowest risk borrower is the federal government. As fiscally irresponsible as the people in our government may sometimes be, we know that they will pay what they owe. How? The government can always raise taxes to cover their debt, or they can print more money (which I suppose is really just another form of fiscal irresponsibility). It is for this reason that the yield on treasury bills—government bonds maturing in less than a year—is often referred to as the *risk-free rate*.

On the other hand, corporations don't have the luxury of printing money, so some can and will default on their loans. A rating system was developed to help investors determine the risk of defaults, and consequently, the appropriate interest rate to charge a company when they borrow. Credit rating agencies assign *ratings* to all bonds when they are issued and monitor developments during their lifetime. For example, Standard & Poor's and Fitch will assign a **AAA** rating to a borrower with outstanding credit, assign a **BBB** to borrowers who are considered "investment grade," and give a **BB** rating or lower when an borrower is high yield or of lower quality. The higher the risk that the borrower may not be able to repay what they owe, the higher the interest rate that they will have to pay for the use of the money.

**Call Risk or Prepayment Risk.** Some bonds have *call features* associated with them and are most often found in corporate and municipal bonds. This means that the borrower may be able to prepay the principal before the bond matures. To compensate the investor, the issuer often pays a little more interest to make up for the increased risk of having that call feature. As you may recall, interest rate increases are accompanied by bond price declines, and interest rate declines go along with bond price increases. This presents a potential problem for the bond investor. Just when the price of my bond is expected to go up (during an interest rate decline), the borrower goes and repays the loan. This is the very reason why I generally avoid callable bonds in my portfolio.

**Inflation Risk.** One of the most sinister risks of investing is that of *inflation risk*. Inflation risk is often called the *silent tax*. We never see it, but it is always at work, destroying the purchasing power of our money. Most bonds do a poor job of protecting us against the ravages of inflation because they are denominated in the currency of this country. In other words, when we buy a bond, we agree to a certain interest payment in U.S. dollars. If the dollar is dropping in value, each payment that the borrower makes is with dollars that are worth less than they were before.

I overheard a conversation one day where a business-owner client of mine was describing this concept to his highly conservative son. The son was advising his father that, if it were his decision, he'd just pay off his old mortgage. To the son's surprise, the father told him that his mortgage was only a couple hundred dollars per month.

"That's it?" the son asked.

Dad replied, "You've got to realize, when I took this out, $200 was a lot of money. I'm taking my time repaying, because every day $200 buys less and less."

Historically, it takes about one hundred years for money to double after inflation in treasury bills. The average rate of return for treasuries is only around .5 percent after inflation. If we figure in taxes our money is, in actuality, most likely going backwards.

To help combat this, some bonds have inflation protection built into them. For instance, the government is now issuing "I-bonds" or *Inflation-bonds*. The idea is that they pay a certain level of interest every year on the principal. When inflation figures are announced, the principal value is adjusted to reflect the inflation number. Two of the main issues regarding these bonds are as follows: 1) The potential fluctuations in value that they can experience and 2) The fact that the borrower and the entity determining the amount of the inflation adjustment are one in the same. The government may have an incentive to keep its borrowing costs down by keeping the inflation numbers artificially low. For these reasons, I would use them very sparingly in a portfolio.

**Reinvestment Risk.** The final type of risk to discuss regarding bonds is *reinvestment risk*. This is the risk that the interest rate at which I can invest my interest payments will be lower that interest rate I'm actually earning on the investment.

If you've been investing long enough, you may remember the good old days when CD's paid sixteen percent, and banks and investment houses gave away toasters if you made a big enough deposit. (Truth be told, those CD rates weren't so great if you consider taxes and the fact that inflation was hovering around the twelve percent range at the time.) As interest rates declined during the 1980s, the interest payments that were reinvested from those CD's had no place to go but down. Once the interest was paid, the borrower had no obligation to pay a high rate on those dollars. Anyone who had calculated their future wealth based on those high rates continuing was more than likely highly disappointed with the end result.

## Bonds and Your Portfolio

Determining the amount of bonds to hold in your portfolio is usually a factor of your time horizon, or how long you plan to invest. Generally, the shorter the time horizon, the greater the percentage of the portfolio that should be dedicated to bonds. Bonds can provide a powerful hedge against stock market downturns, but as you've seen, they contain some fairly formidable risks as well. Later in the book, I will discuss the particulars of choosing the type of bonds for your specific investment objectives.

## Summary

- Before any investor begins to invest, it is important to first develop an understanding of the primary building blocks of an investment portfolio.

- A bond is a tool that is used when a company, mortgagee, or governmental unit borrows money. Bonds are usually issued in even denominations and have a certain period of time before they mature.

- There are three typical maturity ranges associated with bonds: 1) Short term 2) Intermediate 3) Long term.

- Treasury bills are government bonds maturing in less than a year. The yield on treasury bills is often referred to as the risk-free rate.

- Credit rating agencies assign ratings to all bonds when they are issued and monitor developments during their lifetime. The ratings range from AAA to BB or lower. The higher the risk that the borrower may not be able to repay what they owe, the higher the interest rate that they will have to pay for the use of the money.

- Inflation risk is often called the silent tax. We never see it, but it is always at work, destroying the purchasing power of our money. Most bonds do a poor job of protecting us against the ravages of inflation because they are denominated in the currency of this country.

- Some bonds have inflation protection built into them. For instance, the government is now issuing I-bonds, or Inflation-bonds. The idea is that they pay a certain level of interest every year on the principal. When inflation figures are announced, the principal value is adjusted to reflect the inflation number.

- Determining the amount of bonds to hold in your portfolio is usually a factor of your time horizon, or how long you plan to invest. Generally, the shorter the time horizon, the greater the percentage of the portfolio that should be dedicated to bonds.

## Quick Quiz

1. All too often, what is the result when we jump into complex topics but lack an understanding of foundational principles?

2. What is a common way that corporations raise capital?

3. What is a bond?

4. True or False: Many bondholders choose bonds because of their stability; and consequently, they are among the first groups in line to get their money back when the issuer of their bonds runs into financial difficulty.

5. What are the three maturity ranges associated with bonds?

6. True or False: The shorter the amount of time a bond has until it matures, the greater the potential amount of volatility that can be experienced by the investor.

7. It is only one year from the date you made a five-year bond investment, but now you want to sell the bond. Interest rates have gone up in the market. What will you have to do to entice someone to buy it?

8. Who is the lowest risk borrower?

9. What is another phrase for inflation risk, and why is it called that?

10. To help combat inflation, some bonds have inflation protection built into them. One example is "I-bonds." How do they work?

11. What is one of the greatest benefits that bonds provide?

"We learned quite some time ago that the real business of Wall Street often consists of introducing people who shouldn't buy securities to people who shouldn't sell them."

-Wall Street Journal

CHAPTER THREE

# UNDERSTANDING STOCKS

# Understanding Stocks

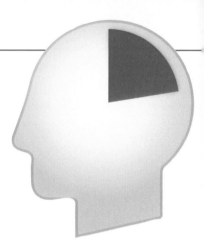

**I**f **you are like most people,** you've heard the stories of great wealth gained and great wealth *lost* by investing in the market. To some, the stock market seems like an endless buffet of possibilities, and as a result, we have long been intrigued with its inner workings. We watch financial news, read the business section, and hear daily reports on the movements of stock prices— what went up and what went down. However, when I ask investors if they really understand how the market works, I usually get a blank stare. If they do answer, it is typically a clichéd response that holds little to no meaning.

If we are going to invest our hard earned money in this thing called the stock market, it is imperative that we know something about how it works. If I bring my car to the mechanic, yet have no clue about what makes a car operate, I am a prime target for a scam. I would be at the mercy of the mechanic and the information he provides me concerning what is wrong with my car and how much it will cost to fix it. The same is true with investing—either we gain a basic understanding of how the market works or become easy prey for the less-than-ethical investment managers or advisors.

## Humble Beginnings

The first organized stock exchange in the United States was created in 1792 by the "Buttonwood Agreement," which was a document signed by twenty-four brokers under a buttonwood tree on Wall Street. In those days, stocks were traded in the local clubs and coffee houses as well as being traded outdoors. According to the *Wall Street Journal*, at one point, there were as many as 250 stock exchanges around the country. It wasn't until 1903 that the New York Stock Exchange (NYSE) relocated to its current address on Wall Street in New York City. Although the NYSE wasn't the first exchange, it is still one of the best known.

Today stocks are traded on exchanges all over the world. The three major exchanges in the United States are the NYSE, the NASDAQ, and the NYSE American (formerly the American Stock Exchange). The vast majority of publicly traded companies are traded through these three exchanges. In the past, stocks were traded at a physical location, but now stocks frequently change hands electronically through networks.

## What is a Stock?

A *stock* is an instrument that shows that you are a part owner of a corporation. This means that, as an owner, you participate in the profits or losses of the company and are a proportional owner of the company's assets. Here is a simple example:

There is a hardware store with 1000 outstanding shares. This means that the company has literally been divided up into 1000 separate ownership pieces (and technically, the company could have 1000 different owners if each person only owned one share).

If you own 50 shares of the company's stock, then you own 5% (or 50/1000th) of the company. Therefore, you get 5% of the profits of the company. When the company grows in value (much like your house going up in value) you are a 5% participant in that as well. If the company pays a dividend or a portion of profits back to its owners, you also get 5% of it.

Let's say that the hardware store made $50,000 in profit. Your piece of the profit pie is $2,500 (or 5% of $50,000). Now, the board of directors you've elected to make big decisions on your behalf is unlikely to send you a check for $2,500. They will likely plow most of that money back into the company for future growth. They might go out and buy a new inventory tracking system to help make them more efficient or purchase a new, faster key-making machine. Either way, their chief aim is to grow the company for the shareholders/owners. Some of the profit money may be used to pay dividends to the shareholders/owners or repurchase company shares, but if nothing goes back into the company, eventually it will lose to the competition.

## Why Own Stocks?

If you ask most people why they invest in stocks, chances are their answer will revolve around the money that can be made in the stock market. However, I believe that the reason to invest in stocks is more subtle—stocks are a great inflation hedge.

*Inflation* is the depreciation of the purchasing power on the dollar. We see this concept manifest itself as prices increase at the gas pumps, grocery stores, car dealerships, and so on. You may remember that stamps used to be thirteen cents in the 1970s, new cars were a couple of thousand dollars, and a new house cost around $25,000. The cost of goods and services are continually rising due largely to inflation.

What most of us don't realize, or think about, is that we actually *own* the entities that are raising prices when we own stocks. To understand the significance of this, we must look at the P/E ratio. You may have heard of the *P/E ratio* before—it is simply a reflection of the amount of money the market is willing to pay for each dollar of earnings from a company. "P" stands for "price" and "E" represents "earnings," so it is the ratio of the market value (or price) per share to the earnings per share.

Stock analysts often use this statistic to make sure the price they are paying for a stock is reasonable. Calculating a stock's P/E ratio is easy. If a stock is selling for $50 per share (P), and has earnings of $5 per share (E), then its P/E ratio is

$$P/E \ RATIO = 50/5 = \mathbf{10} \ (or \ 10/1)$$

This tells us that traders are willing to pay $10 for every $1 in earnings.

Taking a deeper look, we can see why stocks can help protect us against inflation. As mentioned earlier, in the P/E ratio, the "E" in the denominator is "earnings." From accounting class, we learned how to arrive at earnings:

**EARNINGS =**

SALES - COST OF GOODS SOLD - GENERAL OPERATING EXPENSES - INTEREST - TAXES - ETC...

And with this calculation, we'll get down to the company's earnings.

When the dollar depreciates, companies raise their prices to make sure they are getting fairly paid for their products and services. That means the "sales" number in the formula above will go up. Of course, all the other numbers will most likely go up as well. Eventually, the company will make sure the earnings increase—they must in order to stay in business. This will positively affect the price of the stock; therefore, it will provide inflation protection.

For example, if a company has a P/E ratio of 15/1, and the dollar's purchasing power is cut in half, the company in question will start to raise prices. This will drive up the "sales" figure and eventually their earnings will double. All else being equal, the stock price will have to rise to $30 to keep the P/E ratio the same (15/1 = 30/2). As you can see in our example, our stock price doubled when costs doubled. This is not to say that stocks necessarily benefit over the short run from inflationary environments, but in the long run, they protect investors against inflation far better than other investments.

## Stock Prices and the Market

The stock market is largely driven by supply and demand. Thus, stock prices are literally set by a willing buyer and a willing seller agreeing on the fair price for the stock they are trading. There is a formula that can help you get an idea of what kind of information traders use to determine if the price is right for a stock. It is called the *Gordon Growth Formula*, named after Professor Myron J. Gordon of the University of Toronto. It is calculated by the following:

# GORDON GROWTH FORMULA

$$P = D \times (1+G) / (R-G)$$
$$\text{Price} = \text{Dividend} \times (1 + \text{Growth Rate}) / (\text{Cost of Capital} - \text{Growth Rate})$$

Although the model has some flaws, it is quite useful for understanding many of the price movements we see in the stock market.[3] (By the way, there won't be a test on the formula.)

Let's say we have a company with an expected dividend of $1, a cost of capital of 10%, and a growth rate of 5%. The Gordon Growth Model would determine the price as follows:

$$P = 1 \times (1 + .05) / (.10 - .05) \quad P = \$21$$

Thus, the model suggests that we would pay $21 for the stock.

To understand how fresh economic information can move the market, let's take a look at a few real-life headlines and articles, and then we'll see how this news can cause changes in stock prices.[4] Keep in mind that I'm using over-simplified numbers to make the math easy, and I changed the company names to protect the innocent. (Please note: The bold/underlined words used below are my own emphasis, not from the articles):

"**XYZ Company** issued a **weak outlook** amid softness in the U.S. housing market and a broader economic slowdown. Its shares **tumbled**."

If the previous estimate of growth was 5%, we might now conclude that the new number should be somewhat lower. Perhaps growth may be expected to go down to 4% in the future. Here's what happens when we plug in the new number:

Price = Dividend x (1 + Growth Rate) / (Cost of Capital – Growth Rate)
Dividend = $1

Cost of Capital = 10% (based on risk and inflation)

Growth Rate = 4%

Price = 1 x (1 + .05) / (.10 – .04)

Price = $17.50

Our stock has dropped in value from $21 to $17.50 based on some bad news about future growth prospects.

Now let's look at a different set of circumstances, again using a real headlines (but fake numbers):

Optimism on U.S. Economy Spurs a Global Rebound

"Stocks rose around much of the world in the third quarter, recouping steep losses from previous months **as <u>fears</u> about inflation and higher U.S. interest rates <u>moderated.</u>**"

The first thing to notice here is that investors' fears have *moderated* or lessened. This often means that they reduce their cost of capital requirements. In other words, investors can't really demand high rates of return when the risk isn't there. The current owners of the stock would rather continue to hang on rather than accept a price that is too low for their shares.

Remember before that our cost of capital number was 10%. Now we'll assume that it goes down to 9%.

Price = Dividend x (1 + Growth Rate) / (Cost of Capital – Growth Rate)

Dividend = $1

Cost of Capital = 9% (based on risk & inflation)

Growth Rate = 5%

Price = 1 x (1 + .05) / (.09 – .05)

Price = $26.25

In this case, our stock jumped in value (from $21 to $26.50) based on a difference in the perceived risk of investing. We will pay more for stocks when we feel safer, and since we'll pay more, the long-term growth potential is reduced.

## Why Do Stocks Fluctuate?

As you can see, stocks are constantly moving up and down in value based on new information being processed by traders. Investors are always trying to get a handle on what profits are going to be in the future and the related risks involved. If there is good news, stocks will adjust upward to reflect that news. When the news is bad—prices will go down. Since professional traders do the vast majority of buying and selling in exchanges around the world, this information is often reflected in stock prices extremely quickly.

One of the key points that I stress in my workshops is this: Any time you see a need to sell stocks, remember that there is someone out there that wants to buy the stocks you are unloading. The same works in reverse—when you get excited about buying, there is always someone waiting to sell them to you.

## The Cost of Capital

Cost of capital is a fancy term for the rate of return investors require to make an investment. At their core, the capital markets (also known as the stock and bond markets) are giant machines for raising money for companies who need it. Put simply, companies want access to your capital and they are willing to pay for the use of your money. The rate of return you can expect will vary based on the risks involved and the inflation rate—and the higher the risk or inflation rate, the higher the expected return.

When it comes to bonds, the cost of capital is easy to determine. All you have to do is look at the interest rate that the company, government, or other borrower is paying to figure out their cost of capital. If they are paying three percent on their bonds, then their cost of capital is three percent, or $3 per year for every $100 borrowed. In most cases (unless the bond is a variable rate bond), the interest payment will remain the same over the life of the loan. In this case, the lender will receive $30 every year with a $1,000 bond.

With stocks, calculating the cost of capital is not quite that simple. Instead of receiving regular interest payments, the owner of the stock is a participant in the earnings of the company. As mentioned earlier, the board of directors doesn't send you a check for all the earnings every year, but they do often pay dividends. What isn't paid as a dividend goes back into the company—of which you own a part.

With that in mind, we can look at the *P/E ratio* in a whole new light. Historically, the average P/E ratio is around 15.9/1. That means that I'm buying $1 of earnings for each $15.90 I pay. If I turn the fraction upside down (like I did with the bond), I've got a 1 to 15.9 ratio or $1 \div 15.9 = 6.29\%$. (Remember the bond paid $3 for each $100 invested, and I could calculate my interest rate by dividing 3 by 100.)

## A Critical Difference Between Stocks and Bonds

It has often been said that stocks are just bonds in disguise. The difference with the bond interest payment and the earnings that I get with the stock is that I have a fighting chance that the stock's earnings will rise over time. The bond issuer has no obligation to pay me any more interest than they agreed to when they borrowed the money. Therefore, higher returns are possible with stocks due to their potential earnings growth, which is not the case with bonds.

How high has that return been? Historically, large US stocks have provided a rate of return in the ten percent range. To put it a different way, their cost of capital has been around ten percent. If we look at any thirty-year period from the mid 1920's to today, we see that the ten percent varies minimally over this span, and many other asset categories have actually provided higher returns. This is interesting because the period in question contains some pretty ominous events, including The Great Depression, World War II, The Korean War, The Cuban Missile Crisis, The Vietnam War, The Oil Crisis, The Gulf War, The Iraq War and The 2008 Financial Crisis.

## Risks of Investing in Stock

It is often said that there is no return without risk—and we all know this. I doubt anyone would ever invest in a CD again if they knew they could get stock market returns with CD-level risk, but that is not reality. Although stocks tend to protect us against inflation risks, they—of course—present us with other risks.

One risk of investing in stocks is called *non-systematic risk*. This is also known as a *diversifiable risk*. It is the risk of losing money in an individual stock. History is full of examples of companies that have gone bankrupt or had severe drops in value due to circumstances that were unique to those companies. For example, when Kmart went bankrupt, it didn't have a negative impact on other retailers. When GM filed for bankruptcy, that didn't mean that Toyota was going to have problems. Most if the time, a company that goes through reorganization due to bankruptcy will actually cancel their old shares. Stocks can drop in value because of competitive pressures, mismanagement, lawsuits, financial troubles, or any number of issues that affect only the company involved.

One study conducted by a group of esteemed professors found that firm-level volatility (the volatility of individual stocks) from 1962 to 1997 more than doubled, but the volatility of the overall market during that time changed very little.[5] In other words, stocks are more volatile than they used to be—in both directions—but the market doesn't move up and down any more than it used to. This suggests that stocks seem to be offsetting each other. When one company drops dramatically, it is just as likely that another company's stock will shoot up in value. The bottom line is that it takes more stocks to be *truly diversified* in the present- day economy. In fact, one part of the study showed that portfolios with more stocks could have less risk and still end up with greater returns.

The other type of risk involved with stock investing is *systematic risk*. This is simply the upward and downward movement that we see in the market. Going back to my boat analogy, it's like the up and down movement of the ocean. When the tide comes in, all boats rise. When it ebbs, they fall. The biggest difference is that the movement of the market is not even as remotely predictable as ocean currents. To further explain this, think of stocks moving like a school of fish (as if you need another analogy). Sometimes you wonder who's following whom as they go up and down in value.

Market risk can't really be avoided, unless of course you decide not to invest in the market at all. The risk can be reduced somewhat, however, by diversifying across different areas of the stock market.

## Cost of Capital and Risk

As we've already covered, a company's cost of capital is easy to determine with bonds. Simply look at the interest rates on borrowed money to determine their cost of capital. If a company has one foot on a banana peel and the other in bankruptcy court, they are going to pay more when they borrow money than a more stable company.

We can often get a glimpse of a company's cost of capital on the stock side when we look at other financial ratios. For instance, a company's price-to-book value can be a useful tool for this purpose. The concept of book value is simple:

Book Value = Assets – Liabilities

*Book value* is just the value of what a company *owns* minus what they *owe*. Most companies are worth more than the value of their land, buildings, machinery, and other assets minus their debts, so they usually sell for more than their book value. Like the P/E ratio, the price-to-book value is also expressed as a fraction: P/B. If a company is selling at or near their book value, this is a sign that investors don't have much confidence in the company. We will talk more about the practical implications of this later in the book.

The price-to-earnings (P/E) ratio can also be used to help investors understand cost of capital. It has some practical limitations that I will discuss in a later chapter, but it helps make this concept clearer. Since the P/E ratio tells us how much investors are paying for each dollar of earnings, it follows that it also tells us how much the person selling the stock must give away to get your money. (Note: It is only when the company is doing an initial public offering—that is, when the company is raising money by selling stock to the public—that your money actually goes to the company. Most of the time, when we buy stock, our money goes to another investor who is selling their holdings.)

Often, investors get excited about investing in some company that has a product line or service that they like. Perhaps they see big lines every time they go to one of its locations or hear great things about the company's future. What they often fail to realize is that everyone else notices it as well and are paying a premium for each dollar of earnings.

One popular company I've used as an example in my workshops has a current P/E ratio of 50 to 1—let's call it BuyMoreCo. Investors are paying $50 for every $1 of BuyMoreCo earnings. Another less popular company, called LowSalesCo, is selling for $10 to every $1 of earnings.

Here's an interesting way to look at this: The owners/stockholders of LowSalesCo get five times less money for each dollar of trailing (past) earnings. To get $50, an owner of LowSalesCo would have to give up the rights to receive $5 of earnings versus the owner of BuyMoreCo giving up only $1.

All else being equal, LowSalesCo has a much higher cost of capital than BuyMoreCo because their owners have to give away more in profits for each dollar raised (assuming profits don't change over the next year).[6] This should remind us of bond investing. The entity that pays more in interest (pays more dollars for each dollar borrowed) has a higher cost of capital than the entity that pays less interest. The difference in cost of capital can also be seen when we examine the two companies' earnings yields. BuyMoreCo's earnings yield is 1/50 or 2%. LowSalesCo's earnings yield is 1/10 or 10%.

## Uncompensated Risk and the Stock Market

Unless you're a thrill seeker, it is probably unwise to take risks you are not being paid to take (and even then, it may not always be wise). The rates of return that we experience from our stock investments are far more driven by the risks that we are taking than any other factor. However, there are some risks that we are not paid to take. In chapter five, we will discuss how to reduce risk through the use of commingled investment vehicles. These investment alternatives are the primary way that investors can take advantage of all the benefits the stock market has to offer.

Next, we will take a look at one of the primary areas where investors get their information about the investing process—the financial media.

## Summary

- There are two choices in investment education: 1) Gain a basic understanding of how the market works. 2) Be a target for the less-than-ethical fund and investment managers.

- The three major exchanges in the United States are the NYSE, the NASDAQ, and the NYSE American.

- A stock is an instrument that shows that you are a part owner of a corporation. This means that you participate in the profits or losses of the company and are a proportional owner of the company's assets.

- Inflation is the depreciation of the purchasing power on the dollar.

- The price to earnings ratio is a statistic used to make sure the price for a stock is reasonable and helps hedge against inflation.

- The Gordon Growth Formula is used to determine what price is right for a stock. It is calculated by: Price = Dividend x (1 + Growth Rate) / (Cost of Capital – Growth Rate).

- The impact of good or bad news on a stock price is reflected extremely quickly, and most often before the general public even hears the news.

- In the capital markets, the rate of return you can expect will vary based on the risks involved and the inflation rate—and the higher the risk or inflation rate, the higher the expected return.

- The big difference between stocks and bonds is that a bond issuer isn't required to pay you more than the initial interest agreed, while a stock's earnings have the potential to increase over time.

- There are two major categories of risks when investing in stocks: 1) Non- systematic risk (or diversifiable risk), the risk of losing money in an individual stock. 2) Systematic risk, the upward and downward movement that we see in the market.

- We can often get a glimpse of a company's cost of capital on the stock side when we look at financial ratios such as book value, which is the value of what a company owns minus what they owe.

## Quick Quiz

1. What was the name of the document that created the first organized stock exchange in 1792?

2. What are the three major stock exchanges used today in the United States?

3. A_____is an instrument that shows that you are a part owner of a corporation.

4. If there is a company with 10,000 outstanding shares and you own 1,000 of those shares, how much of the company (in percentages) do you own?

5. Name one compelling reason to invest in stocks.

6. The cost of goods and services is continually rising due largely to _____.

7. True or False: The Gordon Growth Formula is useful for understanding many of the price movements we see in the stock market.

8. What are capital markets?

9. What is the major difference between a bond payment and stock earnings?

10. What are the two primary types of risks when investing in stocks?

11. A company's cost of capital is easy to determine with bonds. What must you look at to determine their cost of capital?

12. True or False: If a company is selling at or near its book value, this is a sign that investors have confidence in the company.

CHAPTER FOUR

# THE MEDIA AND INVESTING

# The Media and Investing

**M**any investors view the general media as an unbiased source of information about investing and other financial topics. Magazines, newspapers, television, newsletters and other information sources all claim to give us solid, factual information on what we should do with our money. However, I've seen many portfolios in complete disarray that were formulated based on the information and advice obtained from these sources of mass communication.

The financial media's desire to make good investment decisions for the general public is certainly nothing new, but unfortunately, their track record does not positively reflect these desires. During the market downturn of 2002, I had to reassure investors by urging them to look back at past downturns and show how the financial writers were unable to give investors any meaningful insights to cope with their circumstances. In fact, in a marathon research session at my local library, I found several articles that showed how the financial world has often misled investors. In many cases, the parallels were uncanny. It seemed that there was a link between misleading information from the media and market downturns—so much for unbiased, solid information. 2008 and 2009 were even worse.

## When Knowledge Isn't Power

Despite the commonly held notion that knowledge is power, sometimes the power that comes from an increase in knowledge can have adverse effects. You might ask, "Paul, what is the harm of following financial topics in the general media? I'm just trying to learn about what's going on." The harm is not in listening to the advice and examining its validity; rather, the harm lies in how we react to the information we receive. Even the most well educated investors can easily become ensnared in the misguided, emotionally driven information that they collect from financial reporting outlets.

In May, June, and July of 2006, the United States stock markets (as well as many foreign markets) suffered their worst declines in years. Many credited an increase in oil prices, a decline in real estate, and a general slowdown in economic activity for the downward market movement. The financial news outlets quickly went into high gear, predicting what the future would bring for investors.

Experts reminded investors of the old Wall Street adage "Sell in May and go away." The idea behind this phrase is to sell your stocks prior to the sleepy—and supposedly negative—summer months and return to the market again in the fall. And like many Wall Street adages, this one had data to back it up. The problem was that the data used had been taken in isolation and had no logical, real-world basis. If a more thorough analysis had been done, commentators would have seen that markets actually move up more often than down during the summer months.

What makes this information so convincing is that it is reported after anecdotal information backs it up, and more importantly, after it is too late to respond to it. In other words, most of the market decline commentary occurs after stock prices have already declined. It's like telling you a hurricane is coming after it has already flooded your house. This after-the-fact reporting is just one of the many reasons why media information doesn't always equal quality information.

## Even I Get Depressed

One of my rituals is reading financial publications to prepare for my weekly radio show. During the warm months, I like to sit on the deck, coffee in hand, and read about what's happening (or what *happened*) in the financial markets over the past few days.

On one particular sunny Saturday afternoon, after several sessions of market declines, I found myself getting depressed about the state of the economy and the condition of the market. Nothing could cheer me up or make me feel better about the faltering state of things. I was genuinely concerned about the financial future, and yet, I was supposed to go on the radio and talk my listeners—many of whom were probably thinking of getting out of the market—into hanging on. That was not exactly an easy task when even I was getting antsy. All of the information pouring from the media pointed to dark clouds on the economic horizon. After all, we had been through several years of stock market gains; so surely we were due for a "correction" in the near future.

## Wisdom From My Wife

After reading dozens of stories about the negative state of affairs and commenting on them to my wife, she asked me a simple question that redirected my increasingly negative, even gloomy point of view.

"What do you always tell your listeners?" she asked. "What do you mean?"

My wife responded, "Don't you tell them to ignore the media?"

*She was right.* There I was, looking for some magical prediction that would give me hope that the recent declines would soon reverse themselves. I was searching for a silver lining in the dark cloud that hung over the economic landscape, but nothing was in sight. And the irony was that I teach my students month after month in my workshops that the financial media rarely get things right when it comes to their future forecasts. I knew better, but I was looking for wisdom in all the wrong places.

That day I went on the air and—as I always do and firmly believe—told my listeners to ignore the doom and gloom they were seeing and reading about everywhere they looked. And what happened? Large U.S. stocks increased in value in each of the next eight months.

I suppose the teacher needs to be reminded of the basics sometimes, too.

## The Blame Game

During any market downturn, it is natural for people to look for a scapegoat. We humans seem to inherently search for someone—anyone—to blame when situations take a turn for the worse. The thinking in the financial world is that a third party has to be at fault for all of the misery that investors are going through. One natural target for finger pointing is the scores of crooked people on Wall Street who directly benefit from their misdeeds. The idea is that we would somehow all be better off (and the market would recover) if we could just get rid of these unethical people.

For example, in 2002 the scapegoat targets were large companies like Arthur Anderson and the executives at Enron. Articles in financial magazines like CNN/ Money recommended taking action against corporate malfeasance to restore investor confidence.[7] This—they believed—would drive the markets back up.

I heard the same thing from several worried investors. Their confidence to invest would return if the crooked men responsible for the dips were prosecuted. After all, if investors had no confidence, then they wouldn't buy stocks. If no one wants stocks, then the price will remain depressed. This progression seems logical enough, but my question was, "Has this ever happened before?"

The answer is a resounding "yes" and goes back at least eighty years to one of the most famous periods in stock market history. It was the period between the years 1929 and early 1933—also known as the beginning of the Great Depression. Stocks declined in value by, in many cases, over eighty percent. Formerly successful investors were driven into bankruptcy and forced to sell their possessions at a fraction of their previous value. The media, sensing great dissatisfaction with the stock market, started writing furiously about what it would take to restore confidence in the market. One such article was entitled "Prison for Security Sharpers."[8] The article contained a cartoon illustration depicting Uncle Sam dropping a "Crooked Banker" into prison. This article was a reaction to an actual event where Albert Wiggin of Chase National Bank shorted the stock of his own company—a trading technique that allows people to benefit when a stock goes down in value.

Another article written the same year chastised accountants for giving false information about companies that they were responsible for auditing. The article suggested that accurate financial statements would go a long way in fixing what was wrong on Wall Street.[9] Both articles sounded eerily similar to the drama being played out during the market downturn of 2002. It seems that history truly does repeat itself.

## GIGO: Garbage In Garbage Out

To borrow a term from the computer industry, the effect of this kind of information is predictable—GIGO, or garbage in, garbage out. Given that the public relies so heavily on opinions fed to them by the media, it is easy to see how articles like these written during the Great Depression would have discouraged investors from staying in the market. *Why invest if the outlook is so dim?*

Certainly the one thing that the articles written in both 1933 and 2002 have in common is that they drove investors away just before the markets recovered. For example, an investor pulling out of the large U.S. stocks (as measured by the S&P 500) in April 1933 would have missed out on well over

300% growth in their investments through August of 1937. Similarly, the S&P 500 went up over 28% in 2003, and small U.S. companies (as measured by the CRSP 9-10) went up over 78%. This pattern was repeated again after the 2008 and early 2009 downturn.

Unfortunately, those who listened to the media during these times suffered for it. The reason is quite simple: Investors who react to bad information get poor investment results.

## Irrational Exuberance

During the stock market boom of the nineties, former Federal Reserve Chairman Alan Greenspan made a famous allegation. In December of 1996, he spoke of the exaggerating financial media, and in doing so, coined a new phrase. "But how do we know when ***irrational exuberance*** has unduly escalated asset values?"[10] By saying this, he implied that the writers in the media and investors in general were often guilty of displaying excessive optimism regarding investing—and he was right.

In the late nineties, investors were scooping up stocks in technology growth companies like they were mother's milk. Stories of the great wealth that could be gained from investing in rapidly growing companies were at every turn. Diversification and calls for prudence in investing were often being blatantly ignored as the *old-fashioned* ways of doing things. The result was that many investors saw their portfolios drop by as much as 80%. In contrast, well-diversified portfolios lost little—if any—value during this time.

Why did investors and their advisors make such large errors in judgment? A large part of the answer may lie with the information being dispensed by the financial media. Here are a few examples of headlines that appeared in major financial publications in the late nineties:

- "Ten Reasons to Turn to the Web." *Investor's Chronicle*, August 27th, 1999

- "Internet: The Safest Bet Around." *Forbes*, July 5th, 1999

- "Decade's Hottest Stocks Reflect Hunger for Anything Tech" *Los Angeles Times*, December 28th 1999

THE MEDIA AND INVESTING   63

These headlines made it seem prudent to jump on the cyberspace bandwagon and join the party. However, the result was devastating to investors who heeded the siren's call.

## The Death of Equities

One of the most difficult times for U.S. investors in recent history was the period between 1966 and 1982. This was the period in economic history that included the OPEC oil embargo years. I remember waiting in long lines to fill up the gas tank and experiencing dramatic increases in gas prices. People were terrified that the world was running out of "Black Gold," while real gold (the metal) rose to a price of over $800 an ounce.

At the height of the uncertainty in August of 1979, *BusinessWeek* ran a cover story entitled, "The Death of Equities." It highlighted how inflation was "destroying the stock market." The article began by pointing out how seven million shareholders had "defected from the stock market since 1970," and pension plans had "been given the go-ahead to shift more of their money from stocks—and bonds—into other investments." The article also pointed out that younger investors were completely avoiding stocks.

If investors had any inclinations about a coming stock market recovery, surely their hopes were dashed after reading this article. The logic backing their belief that the stock market seemed doomed to the scrap heap of investing history appeared seamless. Profits were an illusion because companies wouldn't be able to raise prices fast enough to keep up, and depreciation methods caused taxes to eat up money that should have gone into capital investing. Investors knew from history that inflation only led to further economic decay. Investors and companies alike had more incentives to utilize bonds rather than stocks. The article even included quotes by a noted professor of economics from a highly respected source—Yale University—to explain why it would take years for any recovery to occur.

So what happened? Was the article correct in its prediction of the demise of stocks? Over the next ten years, large U.S. stocks (as measured by the S&P 500) averaged over 17% per year. From September of 1979—only one month after the article date—through August of 1980, the market delivered an 18.11% return.

Given those numbers, it looks like some staff writer may have lost his job.

*BusinessWeek* had delivered a premature obituary that may have likely driven many investors from the stock market—just when they should have held on.

## Betting On An Old Horse

We've all seen the magazine headlines as we wander through the aisles at the local grocery market:

- Ten Funds for the Year Ahead

- Eight Stocks You Must Own Now

- *How the President was Abducted by an Alien* (Just making sure you're paying attention)

The message seems to be that we must make a drastic change in our investment direction based on the in-depth research of the author of the article. However, the truth is probably closer to this: The author has done in-depth research on what the best funds would have been if you had invested in them three to five years ago. In essence, the author is telling us to play the lottery with last week's winning numbers.

One of my favorite activities on my radio program is to take the recommendations of the experts and show what would have happened over the following year if we had acted on them. In the vast majority of instances, the funds in question went on to underperform—and often quite drastically—the areas of the market in which they were invested. While articles like these may sell magazines, they rarely make for good investment advice. Studies (the kinds of studies that don't get quoted in investment magazines) show that the best funds from the past rarely go on to outperform in the future.

## Real Money - Real Mistakes

One of my favorite articles from the 2008 (technically late 2007, 2008 and into 2009) market downturn appeared in *Reuters* on April 16th of 2009. The article was entitled "NYSE CEO seen cautious over March rally." Here is a guy that should be able to tell us how everything works and what is going on. The head of the world's biggest stock exchange, the article said, commented that the "real money" investors sat out the March rally and were waiting for another one in June or July.

What if these "sophisticated" investors did indeed sit things out until June? They would have missed a 25.83% return in the S&P 500 and over 53% in returns in small company stocks.

## Why Are We Still Listening?

At this point you might be saying, "Okay, I'm convinced that the media isn't great at dispensing investment advice. So why do they continue to do what they do?" The answer has more to do with marketing than anything else. If they didn't have the hot new fund manager, hot stock, market prediction or new investment strategy to discuss, it would be rather difficult to fill an entire magazine or have any topics for discussion month after month. After all, writing about the prudent management of investment portfolios would get boring rather quickly, and further subscriptions would, quite frankly, be unnecessary. And if no one is looking at your magazine, it follows that advertisers would lose interest quickly, and given that ad sales are the lifeblood of any publication, publishers must give the readers what they think they want in order to keep the ad revenue streams flowing.

As we discussed in a previous chapter, consumers tend to buy based on emotions and instincts. It would be the death of any magazine that decided to market to the cognitive mind—the part of our brain that deals with facts, figures, and statistics. People don't respond to reason, and the media knows this. So they feed us what drives us to act—the feelings of fear, greed, and other emotions.

In short, I believe the media's desire to be the most current, insightful, cutting-edge provider of information is inconsistent with the tenets that make up prudent investing. As one active manager once said to me, "Oh Paul, the stuff you teach just isn't sexy."

And to that I say if arriving at retirement completely broke is what you're after, then you can have sexy.

## Summary

- It seems there is a link between misleading information from the media and market downturns; and it often serves us to ignore the media.

- Even the most well educated investors can easily become ensnared in the misguided, emotionally driven information that they collect from financial reporting outlets.

- The problem with information from the media is that much of the data used is taken in isolation with no logical, real-world basis.

- After-the-fact reporting is just one of the many reasons why media information doesn't always equal quality information.

- Alan Greenspan famously implied that the writers in the media and investors were guilty of displaying excessive optimism regarding investing during the mid-nineties that he called "irrational exuberance." Yet, the public still relies heavily on opinions fed to us by the media.

- Past performance recommendations are given based on in-depth research on what the best funds would have been if you had invested in them three to five years ago. In essence, the media is telling us to play the lottery with last week's winning numbers.

- The reason for the misleading info is really about marketing more than anything else. Magazines and news programs need the hottest new stock picks to fill up precious time and space and sell more copies.

- Prudent fund management may not be sexy, but it's better to retire in peace with a secure nest egg than to practice sexy investing.

## Quick Quiz

1. Sometimes knowledge isn't power. How can this be so?

2. What does the old adage, "Sell in May and go away" mean? And is it true?

3. What's often the best thing to do with the "doom and gloom" information from the media in regard to your investments?

4. Why still invest if the economic outlook according to the media is so grim?

5. What phrase did Alan Greenspan use in 1996 to describe what he saw as excess optimism on the part of investors and the media?

6. Focusing on the top investments in previous years is analogous to playing the lottery with _____ _____'s winning numbers.

7. Why does the media continue to dispense advice that is not reliable or proven?

## CHAPTER FIVE

# COMMINGLED
# INVESTMENT VEHICLES

# Commingled Investment Vehicles

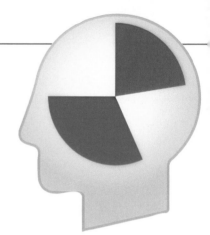

**O**ne of the biggest fears that most prospective investors seem to share is the fear that they will lose all of their hard-earned wealth when they invest. We've all heard horror stories of investors who were set to retire only to have their stocks plummet in value, causing them to delay or even completely cancel their plans for the Golden Years. It's sad to see because it can be prevented through proper diversification.

*Diversification* is one of the oldest investing concepts known to mankind. In the Biblical book of Ecclesiastes, Solomon advised that one should, "Divide your portion to seven, or even to eight, for you do not know what misfortune may occur on the earth."[11] This is great advice from the wisest and wealthiest king to ever live, and today, we would be well advised to invest our wealth in an even broader fashion than Solomon first suggested. With the wide array of investment vehicles at our disposal, there is no reason why we should put our holdings at great risk of a catastrophic loss through a simple lack of diversification.

## Risk Versus Return

Given all that we know about the benefits of diversification, why then do investors take on the risk of investing in small numbers of stocks and narrow segments of the market? It is largely due to a misunderstanding of the risk/return trade-off. Investors intuitively understand that greater returns are possible when they take greater risks, but what they don't realize is that many of the risks they take aren't actually expected to produce higher returns. Put simply, higher risk does *not always equal* a higher return, especially when those high risks are uncalculated or poorly executed.

Imagine that you are planning a short plane trip to a nearby city. A friend of yours has a beautifully restored World War I biplane at the local airport and offers you a ride. When you arrive, you determine that you have two choices on where to ride on the plane. The first choice is in the passenger seat, while the second is on the airplane's wing. Though some may choose to hang on the wing, we can probably all agree that your likelihood of arriving at your destination any faster would not be enhanced by this highly dangerous choice. It is simply a risk that is unlikely to have any great reward attached to it (that is, outside of bragging rights).

The same is true of investing in the stock market. There is no greater expected return of investing in a single large U.S. growth stock than there is investing in all U.S. large growth companies. Remember, investing is all about the cost of capital. When you invest, you are letting others have use of your money— or your capital. They want to pay you as little as possible while you want to be paid as much as possible. So the old adage is true: *Don't put all your eggs in one basket.* What happens when that basket breaks, and the eggs (your capital) are lost from one fatal mistake? Why not give yourself the greatest chance for success by spreading your eggs out among many baskets; so that if one breaks, you know you can survive to face another day without having lost your retirement on a single decision.

## The Difficulty of Self-Diversification

When reviewing individual investment portfolios, I often see individual stocks. Many times the investor tells me that the broker advising him was trying to help him set up his "own mutual fund." In other instances, investors gravitate to individual stocks hoping to find and own the next Microsoft, Amazon or another company that will hit it big. It's a great thought, but the problem is that individual investors rarely have the resources to become properly diversified on their own. To illustrate, let's look at a simple example:

Let's say I want to get completely diversified in the largest U.S. companies— the S&P 500. If I want to own all 500 stocks, the first thing I would consider is how to buy them as inexpensively as possible. This would necessitate buying them in "round lots," or one hundred share units. Trading in smaller units, or "odd lots," is more expensive. Let's assume that the average share price is $50. Based on these numbers, the amount of money I would have to invest would be:

**500 companies x $50 per share x 100 share units = $2.5 million**

This amount would allow for diversification in the area of large blend stocks. Now we have to consider large value stocks, small blend stocks, small value stocks, international large, international small, etc. Obviously, most investors would have a hard time coming up with the first $2.5 million, let alone the substantial amount of money needed to cover the other categories. The bottom line is that this type of investing is simply not feasible for the average individual investor.

## What is a Commingled Investment Vehicle?

So, if we can't safely diversify on our own without having millions in capital, what choice do we individual investors have? One solution is a commingled investment vehicle. A *commingled investment vehicle* is just a fancy term for an investment product that is the result of pooling multiple investors' assets. It's like throwing a slew of different items in a single bucket of which a large group of people all has ownership. Common examples of commingled investment vehicles are:

- Mutual Funds
- Variable Annuity Sub-accounts
- Exchange Traded Funds (ETFs)

By pooling our assets with other investors, we can achieve much higher levels of diversification than we can on our own, and everyone who owns the commingled vehicle will own the assets in the same exact proportions. This type of investing also allows the individual investor to take advantage of the thousands of stocks (in the United States alone) from which we have to choose. If we look at the cost of owning all of them, we can easily see why commingling is such a popular concept.

**Unsystematic Risk.** The primary risk that commingled investment vehicles are designed to alleviate is unsystematic risk. *Unsystematic risk* is the risk of loss that comes with investing in an insufficient number of different investment vehicles. For example, there is a much greater likelihood that one large U.S. company could go bankrupt than there is that all large U.S. large companies would go out of business. There is also a greater level of volatility with individual stocks that we don't see with the market as a whole. Since we are not expected to gain any additional return from taking this risk, it makes little sense to subject ourselves to it.

The graph below shows the volatility of individual stocks versus the market at large. The areas shaded with blue show the greater swings in value that individual stocks are often subject to, while the market as a whole tends to stay within a more controlled range of returns. This graph helps explain why another term used to describe this risk is *uncompensated risk*. Quite simply, we shouldn't take risks that we're not paid to take.

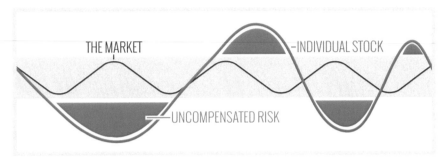

This graph is a good illustration of how adding stocks is a good way to reduce unsystemic risk in your investment plan.

## A Look at Mutual Funds

The most common type of commingled investment alternative is the *mutual fund*. Most mutual funds are of the open-ended variety. An *open-end mutual fund* means that new shares are constantly being offered to the public. When you see an advertisement on TV or in a magazine, it is typically referring to an open-end mutual fund.

Mutual funds come in a dizzying number of varieties. There are mutual funds that invest in stocks, bonds, real estate, preferred stocks, options, and virtually any other investment vehicle you can imagine. Many mutual funds invest in a combination of these categories. I will go into some detail regarding the pros and cons of funds that use a mixture of investment vehicles later in the book.

There are many ways that investors can buy mutual funds for their portfolios. The biggest difference between the alternatives usually comes down to alternative pricing methods. A term used to describe these differences is *share classes*.

Share classes are sometimes identified with a letter at the end of the fund name. For example, you might see a fund listed as the Skybound Growth Fund R. That just signifies how the fund charges investors for investing. Some funds charge an upfront commission that is paid to the broker who sold it to you. Some have fees for leaving or pulling your money out of the fund before a predetermined time period is up and some have no front or back-end "loads" at all. These funds are typically referred to as no-load funds.

## No Load Funds

I typically recommend that investors use no-load funds for two simple reasons. One is that it can take some of the friction out of the investing process. When managing an investment portfolio, it often becomes necessary to sell some or all of one fund and buy another for reasons that we will explore later. If I have to pay a new fee every time I sell one thing and buy another, I will end up giving away a lot of my investment fund. I'm nice, but not *that* nice.

Another reason I prefer no-load funds is their transparency. The management fees are easy to discern and it takes fewer math skills to figure out what you're paying. I also like the idea that there are no commissions being paid to a salesperson/advisor. I believe commissions can cause the following problems:

- There is often an incentive to do something when *nothing* is the right thing to do.

- There is an incentive to offer products that pay higher commissions to the advisor, unbeknownst to the investor.

- There is the incentive to recommend what the investor will buy, rather than what they *need*.

*Incidentally, these problems are very common in the annuity industry as well. Annuities are recommended far more often than they should be due to their generous commission structure.*

## More on Fees

When it comes to fees, it is often just a matter of *when* you will pay, not *if.* That is why it is a good idea to study these expenses as well as any tax ramifications before making rapid decisions on what to do with your funds. When studying expenses, it is also important to note that despite which class of mutual funds you choose, there is no reduction in management fees regardless of the size of the account. Large accounts pay the same percentage of assets for management as a smaller investor would have to pay. However, some fund companies will automatically switch you to lower cost fund share classes when your account reaches certain levels such as fifty or one-hundred thousand dollars.

In some cases you can benefit from being part of a large group of investors and get access to "institutional" no-load funds. These are funds that often require large minimum deposits to gain entry - sometimes five-million dollars or more. This is sometimes seen in large company 401(k) plans and can be a benefit of working with an advisor. Advisors will often pool client money to get access to these types of funds. Not only are the fees often lower, they can benefit from other cost advantages. We'll cover that in more detail in chapter 9.

## Mutual Fund Prospectuses: Companion or Kindling?

One of the biggest complaints I hear from investors involves the complexity of the mutual fund prospectus that they receive in the mail when they invest. Many will tell me that they just throw them in the trash or use them to start fires at their campsite. However confusing it may seem, the prospectus is an important tool that should be used to choose investments for your financial future. In the days before prospectuses, investors blindly put their money in investment vehicles. They had little way of knowing where their money was going and determining the costs involved. This was often disastrous, as count-less people put money into investments that were overpriced and expensive.

Many commentators believe that the huge losses incurred by investors during the Great Depression were suffered—in part—due to an overall lack of quality, accurate information available to investors. Therefore, even though many investors don't pay attention to the information in prospectuses, you can take great comfort in knowing that enough people do pay attention that it protects everyone.

## Prospectus Disclosure

There are several pieces of critical information contained in mutual fund prospectuses of which you, as an investor, should be aware. The prospectus is your first line of defense in making sure that each segment of your overall portfolio is being managed in a manner that is consistent with your investment philosophy and overall objectives. While I will spend a significant amount of time covering the prudent management of your investments later in the book, here are some of the main pieces of information that you will find in a prospectus:

**Objective.** This section details the types of securities that the fund can invest in, as well as the primary objective of the fund. This information is useful in determining if the fund can be used to effectively carry out the asset allocation you have chosen. *One word of warning:* If the fund has too much flexibility regarding the areas of the market in which it can invest, you may want to avoid it. Too much flexibility can be a sign that the fund manager likes to engage in market timing. As I will later cover, this is a process that often results in lower long-term returns.

**Expenses.** The expenses of a mutual fund are often broken down into several categories in a prospectus. Some of the categories you may find listed are *front- end sales charges* (fees for getting in), *back-end sales charges* (fees for getting out too early), *management fees* (fees charged while you are invested in the fund—expressed as a percentage of the account balance), *distribution fees*, and other related expenses. As we will see, many of the expenses of investing aren't explicitly disclosed in the prospectus. Understanding expenses is a critical part of investing in a mutual fund because excessive expenses can have a substantial impact on the growth of your investments.

**Performance.** The prospectus also outlines the past performance of the mutual fund. Unfortunately, it is important to note that investors sometimes use this information improperly. Even though the fund must disclose that past performance is *no guarantee* of future results, many people choose a fund as if it stated that the fund would produce the same high returns as it has historically. We will examine how and when to use performance data in the selection of a fund in a later chapter.

**Shareholder Information.** This section of the prospectus tells you how to buy and redeem shares of the fund. You can also discover the minimum amount of money it takes to buy shares and what the minimum account value is for each fund investor.

**Other Information.** Reading a prospectus can be an eye-opening experience for an investor. It is not unusual to read disclosures in the prospectus regarding payments that the fund makes to certain brokerage firms for recommending the fund. You may also find that the fund reserves the right to increase expenses and change the objective of the fund without consulting the shareholders. When they tell you to read a prospectus carefully, you may want to heed the advice.

As you can see, the world of commingled investments can be complex and confusing. The industry is largely driven by marketing and sales, but the process of commingling can be one of your best tools in making sure your investments are protected against having too many of your eggs in one basket.

## Summary

- One of the biggest fears that most prospective investors seem to share is the fear that they will lose all of their hard-earned wealth when they invest.

- Diversification is one of the oldest investing concepts known to mankind, dating back to Biblical times.

- Due to the large amount of assets required, self-diversification is simply not feasible for the average individual investor.

- A commingled investment vehicle is an investment product that is the result of pooling multiple investors' assets. Common examples of commingled investment vehicles are mutual funds, variable annuity sub-accounts, and exchange traded funds (ETFs).

- Unsystematic risk is the risk of loss that comes with investing in an insufficient number of different investment vehicles.

- The most common type of commingled investment alternative is the mutual fund. Most mutual funds are of the open-ended variety. An open-end mutual fund means that new shares are constantly being offered to the public.

- The biggest difference between the mutual fund alternatives usually comes down to various pricing methods called share classes. The share classes are often identified by letters after the fund name or may be No-Load funds.

- The mutual fund prospectus is your first line of defense in making sure that each segment of your overall portfolio is being managed in a manner that is consistent with your investment philosophy and overall objectives.

- Various sections of a prospectus include: Objective, expenses, performance, and shareholder information.

## Quick Quiz

1. What is one of the oldest investing concepts known to mankind?

2. Why do investors take on the risk of investing in small numbers of stocks and narrow segments of the market?

3. If we can't safely diversify on our own without having millions in capital, what choice do individual investors have?

4. What are some common examples of commingled investment vehicles?

5. What is another term for unsystematic risk, and why is it called this?

6. What is the most common type of commingled investment?

7. What type of fee is charged upfront when buying a mutual fund, and what does this fee typically pay for?

8. What are two potential problems with commission-based investing?

9. When it comes to mutual funds, it is often just a matter of _____ you will pay, not _____.

10. As confusing as it may seem, what is an important tool that should be used to choose investments for your financial future?

CHAPTER SIX

# THE FIRST MYTH: STOCK PICKING

# The First Myth: Stock Picking

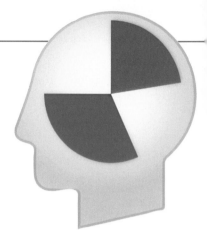

**N**ow that you have an understanding of the way that markets work, how the media tends to mislead investors, and what commingled investment vehicles are, it is time to delve into the *myths of investing*. There are four basic categories of investing myths that will be discussed in the next several chapters. These myths tend to go largely undetected by investors because the financial industry has so much to gain by their perpetuation. Here are the four myths of investing:

1. The Success of Stock Picking

2. Belief in Market Timing

3. Relying on Past Performance

4. The Idea that Costs Don't Matter

Investing based on these myths causes investors to have drastically reduced returns and threatens their very retirement security, and yet their influence in every corner of the investing world is never ceasing. The only chance we have to escape them is to take a close look at how they are used—and why they don't work.

As the old saying goes, *"Know thy enemy".*

## The Basics of Stock Picking

If you've ever gone to a gathering of friends, turned on a TV, or spent any time with other human beings, you have probably been exposed to the concept of *stock picking*. The idea is that an investor or an investment advisor utilizes their skill and knowledge to determine which stocks have the greatest promise of delivering good returns in the future.

It's the hunt for the next Apple, that stock that will catapult us into the category of the rich and maybe even the famous. We've all heard the stories of fortunate investors who put just a small amount in a little start-up firm and retired with untold wealth. It stirs the imagination to consider how our lives could be different if that happened to us. The problem is that Wall Street tends to benefit from our exaggerated belief in our stock picking aptitude far more than we, the individual investors, do.

## Mutual Funds Gone Wild

The number of stock mutual funds continues to grow at unprecedented rates over the past several years. As we have all heard, the Baby Boomer generation is moving into retirement and needs a place to stash their hard-earned retirement money. The most logical choices are often mutual funds because of the ease of investing and the relative availability of funds in workplace retirement plans. Unfortunately, the competition between fund companies has caused most fund families to gamble with their investors' money in order to gain the spotlight.

Studies show that investor money is far more likely to gravitate to funds that have beaten their peers. Because of this, fund managers feel tremendous pressure to find the stocks that will give them superior returns. The result is that the average stock mutual fund turns its portfolio over at a rate of nearly 100% per year. This means that funds are selling literally every stock and replacing them every calendar year. The scary part is that average investors are often completely unaware that this activity is taking place—but they are paying for it regardless.

## The Failure of Stock Picking

If actively selecting the best stocks and figuring out which companies would make the best investments were a valid strategy, it would stand to reason that mutual fund managers using this tactic could significantly add value above market returns. However, this is not what we observe when examining actual returns. Studies reveal that mutual funds containing actively selected stocks routinely underperform the areas of the market in which they are invested. It is important to understand this, because mutual fund families and managers of stock funds try to create the impression that we should hire them to help us find the best stocks and avoid the bad ones.

One study by SPIVA ending in 2016 showed 88.3% of actively managed funds failed to match the returns of the S&P 500[12] over the previous five-year period. The numbers were even worse for small company stock funds. Against the S&P 600 small cap index, 86.7% of managers fell short over the same period.

The idea at work behind this myth is that supposedly the investment markets are not properly pricing some stocks, and those inappropriate pricings can be detected by well-informed investors. It's almost as if the manager is saying to investors, *"Psst, I know something about these companies that no one else does, and what I can do is buy their stocks cheap today, and then sell them for a lot more when the market discovers my secret."* What's amazing is that most investors actually believe this is true.

## Darts Anyone?

To illustrate the failing of active stock management, I used to perform a little experiment with the attendees in my workshops. Before starting the workshop, I would ask each person to throw darts at the large company stock tables I had posted in my classroom. Nearly every time we conducted the experiment, my dart-throwing students beat the professional mutual fund managers' they were competing against. (I finally gave up the experiment because my walls were taking a beating. Some people just have bad aim.)

This experiment is like the one John Stossel performed for *20/20* viewers several years ago. He still repeats it from time to time with similar results. In a particularly memorable segment, Stossel took the investment industry to task when his dart throws beat the performance of nine out the ten biggest brokerage firms. Stossel said, "We wanted to ask the brokerage firms about this. Why should anyone listen to their important sounding advice, given their poor track record? That's what we wanted to ask them, but not one of the big New York brokerage firms would agree to talk to us about this. I guess I could understand why."[13]

## The Muddled Media

The financial media tends to keep the successful stock picking myth alive through their constant focus on yesterday's winners. No matter what is going on in the investment markets, magazines, financial newspapers and television shows seek out those investment professionals who managed to accurately forecast the latest market movements or uncover what became the hot stock of the day.

One such example is investment manager Bill Miller who used to manage the Legg Mason Value Trust. Miller gained notoriety when he outperformed the S&P 500 for 15 straight years. Due to the tremendous fanfare that the media created as they lauded his amazing feat, the fund attracted large amounts of investor dollars. The success, however, didn't last. A quote from Money magazine says it all: "A $10,000 investment in Miller's Opportunity Trust fund at the end of 2006 shrank to just $4,815 by the end of 2011, thanks in part to big bets on hobbled financial stocks, according to Morningstar.com."[14]

What is amazing to me is that the story doesn't end there. A 2017 Headline from CNBC states: "Legendary investor Bill Miller is killing it again, thanks to a clever bet on Apple." That led me to review the performance of the fund referenced in the article — under the S&P 500 by over 3% per year for 10 years.   The article was completely focused on recent performance and ignored the bigger picture.

## Individual Investor Performance

Individual investors don't fair any better. While data on individual investor returns can be hard to find, one I saw in 2017 illustrates this point well. Hart Lambur, co-founder and CEO of Openfolio, shared data on member returns. Openfolio is a social network with more than 70,000 members who share their portfolio holdings. According to Lambur, the average investor had a gain of roughly 5% in 2016[15]. Over the same period of time, the S&P 500 returned nearly 12% and small companies, as measured by the Russell 2000, returned over 21%[16]. While people may brag at cocktail parties about their successes in the market, these numbers paint a different picture.

Achieving long-term success in the world of investing involves far more than some lucky guesses based on a "hunch" that a certain stock will soar. That type of stock picking—rapid-fire selections based on a "get rich quick" mentality or "insider" information—does not usually end well. Stock prices, like any other element in business, move in direct relation to shifts in supply and demand. So then, the practice of stock picking becomes extraneous because, ultimately, the economy and markets say where the stocks will go—and not the individual investor or fund manager. A few stocks will always be outliers whose results will under-or over-perform the market segment to which they belong (like the S&P 500 or Russell 2000), but the rest seldom grow at significantly higher speeds.

Finally, stock picking is a myth based on unfounded hunches about making quick profits instead of using logic, reason, and research. The bottom line is that it is dangerous to even hint around the idea that anyone can go from rags to riches simply by using some special skill in picking the right stock. One lesson life should have taught us by now is that there is no such thing as easy money. Yes, there are the few who get lucky, but luck is not a wise investment strategy for those who actually want to retire one day.

## Summary

- There are four categories of investing myths: 1) The success of stock picking 2) Belief in market timing 3) Relying on past performance 4) The idea that costs don't matter.

- Investing based on these myths causes investors to have drastically reduced returns and threatens their very retirement security, and yet their influence in every corner of the investing world is never ceasing.

- The myth of stock picking assumes that an investor or an investment advisor utilizes their skill and knowledge to determine which stocks have the greatest promise of delivering good returns in the future.

- Studies reveal that the mutual funds containing actively selected stocks routinely underperform the areas of the market in which they are investing. One study found that actively managed funds cost investors part of their returns in almost every asset class or area of the stock market.

- The financial media tends to keep the successful stock picking myth alive through their constant focus on yesterday's winners.

- Achieving long-term success in the world of investing involves far more than some lucky guesses based on a gut feeling that a certain stock will soar. That type of stock picking does not usually end well.

- Stock picking is a myth based on unfounded hunches about making quick profits instead of using logic, reason, and research.

## Quick Quiz

1. What are the four basic categories of investing myths?

2. What is the only chance we have to escape the myths of investing?

3. What is stock picking?

4. Who benefits from stock picking?

5. What has the fierce competition among mutual funds caused fund families to do?

6. What is typically true of actively managed funds?

7. The financial media tends to keep the successful stock picking myth alive through their constant focus on _____'s _____.

8. True or False: Stock prices are not directly related to shifts in supply and demand.

9. Stock picking takes a process that should be based on realistic risk and reward and throws _____, _____, and _____ out the window.

"October: This is one of the peculiarly dangerous months to speculate in stocks.

The others are July, January, September, April, November, May, March, June, December, August and February."

—Mark Twain

## CHAPTER SEVEN

THE SECOND MYTH: MARKET TIMING

# The Second Myth: Market Timing

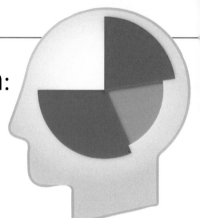

Just as stock-picking behavior illustrates investors' beliefs that there are mis-pricings in individual stocks upon which they can capitalize, the myth of market timing assumes that entire segments of the market are mispriced. Simply defined, market timing is any attempt to change the mix of your portfolio based on a prediction or forecast of the future. After all, if I am changing the mix of my portfolio, I must assume that one area will do better than another area in the near term. In its purest form, market timing may involve moving all of one's money from stocks into cash in anticipation of a market downturn; or conversely, it may require moving all of one's money to stock in the expectation that stocks will rally.

## Where are the Success Stories?

The temptation to time the market is almost overwhelming to some investors. The wealth that could be gained with this magical ability is staggering. I looked at data from the Center for Research in Security Prices at the University of Chicago and calculated what $1 would have grown to if invested in the entire U.S. stock market and got the market return during "up" months, but missed the negatives when the market went down. With perfect market timing, my dollar would have grown to over *one-hundred twenty-two billion dollars*. This compares the $1 "only" growing to about $6,027 from 1926-2017 if invested and left alone during both market ups and downs.[17]

Those are indeed remarkable results—*but is it even possible to time the market in this manner?* Multiple studies on the topic strongly suggest the answer to that question is a resounding "no." Too many people have tried, and con-tinue to try, without any long-term success. According to data from Morningstar®, investors in actively managed funds only captured 71% of the fund's returns due to lack of discipline and a desire to time the market. Investors in international markets faired even worse, capturing only an estimated 33% of returns.[18] Add to that the general under-performance of actively managed funds and we're talking real money.

If market timing worked, the wealthiest people should be able to hire the best market timers out there, right? However, the *Forbes* estimate of the growth in wealth of the "Fortune 400" from 1982 to 2006 is $91.8 billion growing to $1.25 trillion. If the same $91.8 billion grew at the rate of the S&P 500, it would have been worth over $2.1 trillion – not far from double. When an investor attempts market timing, it almost always results in lower returns than a buy-and-hold approach to investing. The investment industry often pays lip service to the idea that market timing is futile despite the fact that most mutual funds (and advisors) engage in a couple different forms of the practice. Two specific examples of market timing are discussed in the following sections: 1) Tactical asset allocation and 2) Style drift.

## Tactical Asset Allocation

*Tactical asset allocation* is a process in which an investment manager or advisor buys several different areas of the market and changes the emphasis based on their market forecasts. For example, an advisor may buy some large companies, small companies, large value companies, international large companies, etc. Then, at some point, the advisor may feel that the large international companies are overvalued and need to be reduced as a holding; or they may determine that large U.S. stocks are poised for a rally and decide to increase their percentage of the portfolio. In either case, the advisor is attempting to time the market. This is very common now with ETF and indexed portfolios, which is ironic because those fund designs usually avoid active management.

The only difference between tactical asset allocation and the simpler form of timing between stocks and cash is in the number of asset categories involved. If the manager really knew that the asset category he was overweighting was headed for a sharp increase, he would put all of the fund investments there. It is no easier to time between ten to fifteen asset classes than it is to time between two—in fact, it is much more difficult.

## Style Drift

*Style drift* is another form of market timing in which a fund manager may start off holding one asset class in the fund and slide into another area of the market, often without the knowledge or consent of the investors. How common is this? A study by S&P/Dow Jones showed that only 25.77% of US large company funds retained their style over a 10 year period ending in 2016.[19] Funds do this primarily for marketing purposes. If a fund can edge out its peers in short-term past performance, then it can gain a competitive advantage (in the short run, at least) in terms of positive press coverage and good ratings.

The industry knows that short-term past performance attracts investors, and that is their main objective—selling mutual funds. Unfortunately for the individual investor, long-term investor success is only a distant secondary goal.

## Why Market Timing Doesn't Work

**News.** The difficulty in timing the market stems from the fact that the stock market responds to new information far too quickly for investors to respond and benefit from that information. Investors often see or read information in the news and try to respond by changing their investments. What they don't realize is that the information they heard has already had an impact on the market because news—whether good or bad—affects market prices as soon as it breaks. If the information is good, owners of stocks will demand a higher price for those stocks than they did before the good news came out. If the news is bad, then the buyers of stocks will reduce the price they are willing to pay. If you found out that the house you are looking to buy has problems with its foundation, you would promptly either reduce your offering price or withdraw the offer altogether. The same principle is true in the stock market.

**Exiting the Market.** Another problem with timing the market has to do with how much it costs to be out of the market when good news hits. We all know those investors who pull their money out of the market when they hear bad economic news. Usually they have contingent plans to start investing again "when things look better." However, a few of my favorite statistics dramatically show how much it can cost to be on the sideline when the tide turns.

To illustrate the effects of temporarily pulling out of the market in anticipation of hard financial times, let's examine the growth of $1 from 1926 through 2017, based on the growth of the S&P 500 over that time period. This period represents 1,104 months. If the investor of $1 remained fully invested during all 1,104 months, the initial deposit would have grown to $7,347 with dividends reinvested. Now, let's say our (very old) investor, a highly unlucky market timer, missed the 48 best months in the market. That means that he was in the market for nearly 96% of the time, but he just missed the top 4% of months. The result would have been a severe reduction in his investment accumulation. The initial investment would have grown to only $21.78. That is close to the growth of $1 in treasury bills over that time period, which would have grown to $20.79.

I also ran data on missing the top 4% of highest returning months in the S&P 500 from the year 2000 through 2017. The result was the same. Missing the top 4% of months due to bad market timing luck erased any returns of stocks above T-bills and then some. Miss a little and you can miss a lot.[20]

Another study from the University of Michigan is based on the time period from 1963 to 2004.[21] In order to measure the effect of market swings, the commissioners of the study looked at the effects of daily and monthly movements of the market over a long time period, and what they found startled them. The study revealed that 96% of the market gains over the thirty-year period were the result of just 0.9% of the trading days.

The underlying problem is that no one really knows when the best days will happen, and ultimately, this uncertainty is what makes market timing so difficult. The events that tend to cause stock and bond prices to move one way or another blindside investors who can only react based on the new information. Any action that an investor takes is most likely going to be far too late and result in unnecessary and wasted spending in order to execute the trade.

## Do *Your* Funds Attempt Market Timing?

Determining whether you have been a victim of a fund manager's attempt to time the market with your money can be difficult. There are a few signs to look for when examining a fund:

**Fund Mix**. One sure sign that your fund manager is attempting to time the market shows up when the fund's mix among different market areas changes year to year. A common example might be regular increases or decreases in the percentage of holdings it carries between U.S. and international stocks. Another example involves the fund manager moving money within various types of companies. This may be difficult to detect unless you are privy to some fairly pricey subscriptions to mutual fund tracking services like Morningstar Direct®, or you are adept at reading annual reports on your funds. An easy shortcut is to look at the mutual fund's prospectus and see if the fund allows such movement among categories. If it does, you can be fairly certain that the manager intends to move money around based on his or her future predictions. This information can usually be found toward the front of the prospectus where the fund's objectives are outlined.

As an example of what the prospectus might say concerning funds subjected to market timing, here is the wording in the investment objective segment of a popular mutual fund: "The fund has the flexibility to invest a limited portion of its assets in companies of any size, to invest in companies whose shares may be subject to controversy, to invest in foreign securities, and to invest in non-equity securities." As you can see, the fund has plenty of latitude to gamble with investors' money.

**Cash Holdings.** Another sign that the fund may be engaging in market timing is a large cash position in the fund. This information can also be found in the fund's annual report. Many mutual funds hold cash while they wait for big news that spells opportunity. The problem, as we have discussed, is that news is digested so rapidly that any action taken will be too little, too late. Since the market tends to move up more than it moves down—and because those upward movements tend to be greater in size than the downward shifts—these large cash holdings put a damper on investment returns. Only the part of the portfolio that is in the market will benefit from the good news. It's like having an eight-cylinder car that is only running on five cylinders—it simply won't perform well.

The abstract of one study said it best when referring to mutual funds and cash holdings: "Aggregate cash holdings do not forecast future market returns, suggesting that equity funds as a whole do not have market timing skills."[22]

Finally, it is important to note that mutual funds might also hold cash to cover unexpected redemptions, or sales, of the fund by investors. Investors tend to panic at the worst times – selling stocks at market lows. Holding cash allows them to buy out these nervous investors without selling stocks at a time when discipline is critical. They are, in effect, accepting the potentially lower return of holding cash, in order to avoid the higher trading cost involved in selling stocks at a bad time. While this is not a visible cost, it is a cost that should be considered when closing investments. More about that later.

## Summary

- The myth of market timing is any attempt to change the portfolio mix based on a prediction or forecast of the future.

- The temptation to time the market is almost overwhelming to some investors. Two specific examples of market timing are discussed in the following sections: 1) Tactical asset allocation 2) Style drift.

- Tactical asset allocation is a process where a mutual fund buys several different areas of the market and changes the emphasis based on their market forecasts.

- Style drift is another form of market timing where a fund manager may start off holding one asset class in the fund and slide into another area of the market, often without the knowledge or consent of the investors.

- The difficulty in timing the market stems from the fact that the stock market responds to new information far too quickly for investors to respond, and ultimately, for investors to benefit from that information.

- One sure sign that your fund is attempting market timing is when the fund's mix between different areas of the market changes from year to year.

- Another sign that the fund might be engaging in market timing is a large cash position in the fund.

## Quick Quiz

1. What is market timing?

2. What assumption does the concept of market timing make?

3. When an investor attempts market timing, it almost always results in what?

4. What are two specific types of market timing?

5. Tactical asset allocation is a process where a mutual fund buys several different areas of the market and changes the emphasis based on their _____.

6. What is the only difference between tactical asset allocation and the simpler form of timing between stocks and cash?

7. What is one of the primary reasons that funds engage in style drift and other forms of market timing?

8. Why doesn't market timing work?

9. What are the signs to look for to determine whether your fund might be engaging in market timing?

## CHAPTER EIGHT

# THE THIRD MYTH: PAST PERFORMANCE

# The Third Myth: Past Performance

**P**  ***ast performance is no guarantee of future results.*** We often see this disclaimer, but do investors and investment providers really act in a way that shows they believe the statement? The answer, of course, is no. Pick up an investment magazine at your local grocery store and, chances are, you will see front-page headlines like "The Ten Best Funds for the Year Ahead," "Funds That Beat the Market," and "The Six Best Undiscovered Funds for Your Portfolio." These headlines are specifically designed to lead you to believe that the fund managers who had great performance in the past are likely to repeat that stellar performance in the future.

The magazines don't have to try hard to make the general public believe this. Reason tells us that it seems logical that managers with great success at choosing the best stocks in the past would have a better than average chance of doing it again in the next round. After all, we look at resumes to find good potential employees, and we ask our friends for their recommendations before choosing a dentist. So, why wouldn't we check out a mutual fund's short- and long-term track record before investing?

## And the Winners Are...

*Kiplinger Personal Finance* magazine runs an annual feature article touting what they call their "Kip 25" list of funds. The list includes no-load (non-commission) funds that are "favorites" due to return history and having below average fees. The editors have done all the research; now all the reader has to do is go and invest in these great funds.

There is no doubt that this type of list attracted many readers who were looking for a fast and simple solution to their investing problems. Unfortunately, the subsequent returns of these winning funds were mediocre at best. It probably never occurred to most readers of *Kiplinger's* list that the primary purpose of the article was not to make us all rich; rather, it was to entice us to buy the magazine so that we would see the advertisements contained inside.

A follow-up article by Nellie S. Huang entitled "How the Kip 25 funds performed," points out some interesting facts that should be red flags to readers.

Huang states that "only a handful" of their US stock fund picks beat the Standard & Poor's 500 stock index over the previous 12 month period. Not to be discouraged, she points out that "the trend is moving in the right direction." Why? The previous year their stock funds actually LOST 9.0% for the period that ended in February 2016.

The same problem plagued the international stock fund choices. Two out of three of their chosen international funds lagged their benchmarks – one by 7.9%.

## Need More Evidence?

To graphically illustrate the inability of fund managers to repeat their performance of the past, consider this graph depicting the number of mutual funds that were in the top 25% of their peer group, in terms of past performance, and how few of them went on to repeat in the following year. As you can see, the top managers of the past rarely repeat as the top managers of the future. *Superior track record* carries little weight.

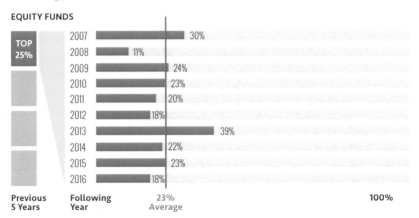

**PAST PERFORMANCE IS NOT ENOUGH TO PREDICT FUTURE RESULTS**

Percentage of top five-year performers that also ranked in the top quartile of annual performance in the following year

**EQUITY FUNDS**

| TOP 25% | | |
|---|---|---|
| 2007 | 30% | |
| 2008 | 11% | |
| 2009 | 24% | |
| 2010 | 23% | |
| 2011 | 20% | |
| 2012 | 18% | |
| 2013 | 39% | |
| 2014 | 22% | |
| 2015 | 23% | |
| 2016 | 18% | |

| Previous 5 Years | Following Year | 23% Average | 100% |

At the end of each year, funds are sorted within their category based on their five-year total return. The tables show the percentage of funds in the top quartile (25%) of five-year performance that ranked in the top quartile of one-year performance in the following year. Example: For 2007, only 30% of equity funds in the top quartile of previous five-year returns through the end of 2006 maintained a top-quartile ranking for one-year returns in 2007. US domiciled open-end mutual fund data is from Morningstar and Center for Research in Security Prices (CRSP) from the University of Chicago. **Past performance is no guarantee of future results. See Data Appendix for more information.**

In a study by Bradford Cornell, Jason Hsu and David Nanigian entitled "Does Past Performance Matter in Investment Manager Selection?" published in the Summer 2017 issue of the *Journal of Portfolio Management*, the authors set out to determine whether selecting managers based on recent outperformance of a benchmark led to superior performance versus that benchmark in the future. A few things were interesting about this study. They looked at top funds in three-year periods and compared the subsequent performance of the top funds of the past with the subsequent performance of the funds that had been significant underperformers previously. Typically, investors, and even pensions, weed out poorly performing funds to ensure that they hold only the best funds going forward.

They even weeded out funds with relatively low levels of assets and high expenses under the theory that these issues would handicap the funds. The result was eye- opening. Not only did the "loser strategy" fund group beat the funds in the middle of the pack ("the median strategy"), they also beat the "winner strategy" funds by 2.28% per year.

This phenomenon is nothing new in the investment world. As you can see from the following quotes, many in the academic community have known for years that investment managers struggle to achieve consistently superior performance:

> "The evidence on mutual fund performance indicates not only that these 115 mutual funds were on average not able to predict security prices well enough to outperform a buy-the-market-and-hold policy, but also that there is very little evidence that any individual fund was able to do significantly better than that which we expected from mere random chance."[23]
> – Michael C. Jenson, Harvard Business School, 1967

> "Contrary to their oft-articulated goal of outperforming the market averages, investment managers are not beating the market; the market is beating them."[24]
>
> – Charles Ellis, 1975

## But Why?

The myths I've outlined have incredible staying power in the investment industry. As we've discussed, one of the reasons for this is they serve the investment industry's marketing efforts incredibly well. Why, then, is it that some of the brightest minds on Wall Street have such a difficult time matching simple market returns?

Ironically, one of the biggest reasons is these professionals are so smart. They are an extremely competitive and intelligent group of people who, because of their level of intellect, tend to keep the market a level playing field. None of them can get a leg up on the others for long. I like to compare this natural law of keeping things in check to driving on a major interstate in rush hour. We've all experienced a traffic jam. As intelligent human beings, our instinct is to find a way to get through the traffic as quickly as we can, which means we must find the fastest lane. We look for slow trucks that can't accelerate quickly enough, as we watch for interstate on- ramps that will add to the number of cars in front of us. We scan the road ahead for the older woman with the "I'm Spending My Kid's Inheritance" bumper sticker because we *just know* she'll be slow. No matter how we plan and calculate, most of us will spend about the same amount of time in life stuck in traffic. Sometimes we may get lucky and choose the right lane, and other times we'll be frustrated with a bad choice. In the end, however, it all evens out.

The same is true with actively picking stocks and timing the market. No one knows when that sure-thing tech company will end up having its top software developer walk out the door to the competition, just like no one knows if the car ahead will suddenly pop a radiator hose. Sure, there will be times when a fund manager gets in the right stock at the right time or manages to buy into what becomes the hottest sector of the market, but there will also be times when the reverse is true.

The bottom line is that since we don't give accolades to drivers who make it through traffic snarls in record time, we shouldn't put investment managers on pedestals when they outperform the market because statistically—and inevitably—there will come a day when they won't.

So far, we've discussed three myths of investing: 1) The belief that stock picking can be a lucrative investment strategy 2) The idea that market timing is a viable option for fund management and, 3) We just debunked the idea of using past performance to pick funds and fund managers. In the next chapter, we'll discuss the final myth of investing. The investment industry wants us to think that the fees and expenses associated with investing don't matter, but we'll uncover how much they do matter and why.

## Summary

- The third myth of investing is using past performance to choose today's picks.

- The disclaimer "Past performance is no guarantee of future results" is everywhere, but investors and investment providers don't act in a way that shows they believe the statement.

- The primary benefit of highlighting past winners is simply to entice us to buy the magazines and watch the programs so that we see the advertisements.

- It's logical to assume that managers with great success at choosing the best stocks in the past would have a better than average chance of doing it again in the next round.

- Just because a manager chose good performers one year doesn't mean he'll do it again the next year. In fact, investment managers constantly struggle to achieve consistently superior performance.

- One of the biggest reasons that investing professionals can't repeat their performances is these professionals are so smart. They are an extremely competitive and intelligent group of people who, because of their level of intellect, tend to keep the market a level playing field.

- We shouldn't put investment managers on pedestals when they out-perform the market because statistically—and inevitably—there will come a day when they won't.

## Quick Quiz

1. What is the most common disclaimer attached to investment products? Does it seem like investors believe it?

2. What is the primary purpose of magazine headlines promising to reveal the big winners?

3. True or False: Top performing managers who consistently perform for at least three years are statistically more reliable than those with only one year of successful returns.

4. According to Charles Ellis, investment managers are not beating the market; the market is _____ _____.

5. What is one of the biggest reasons why investment pros have such a difficult time matching simple market returns?

"If past history
was all there was
to the game,
the richest people
would be
librarians."

-Warren Buffett

CHAPTER NINE

# THE FOURTH MYTH:
# EXPENSES DON'T MATTER

# The Fourth Myth: Expenses Don't Matter

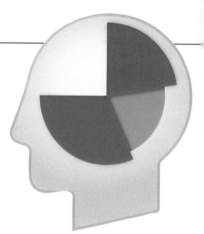

**O**ften times, it seems as though the investment industry says to investors, "Don't worry about the costs, we'll make it up in great performance." From what we've already discussed, this promise is obviously not likely to be true, which leads us to the final myth: The idea that expenses don't matter. You may already be familiar with one of the most quoted sources of expenses with mutual funds—the expense ratio or management fee. This fee is assessed on the balance of your investment in the fund. The fee typically pays for costs associated with the management company, the fund distribution company, the custodian, the transfer agent, attorneys and accountants.

Even if the fund does make an effort to keep management fees low, it often does little to control the hidden trading costs that the fund incurs. Every time a fund manager buys and sells a stock, they must pay for that trade. And each expense—no matter how big or small—can have a dramatic effect on the returns. For example, if a fund has just 2% in excess expenses, it can reduce the accumulation of a single deposit by nearly 37% over a twenty-five year period. Now, let's take a look at some of the less obvious expenses that investors incur when buying mutual funds.

## Bid/Ask Trading Cost

If you've ever traded in your vehicle for a new one, you already understand the concept of bid/ask trading cost. The car dealer offers you a certain sum of money for your old car, and then the dealership sells it to another customer for an increased price. The same thing happens in the stock market. If I want to sell a stock, I can't sell it to a neighbor. I have to go to a brokerage firm grocery store. These stores "make a market" for Crest® toothpaste. In the stock market, this system allows you to sell most stocks almost any time you desire. For example, if you want to sell Walt Disney stock, there is a market maker who will buy the stock. The market maker will then look for another willing buyer to purchase the stock. Obviously, if the stock's price drops after buying it from you, they could lose money on the transaction; so the spread between what they pay you and what they sell it for compensates them for taking the risk of finding the buyer.

Because more effort is needed to fill orders (and therefore more risk is incurred), small companies tend to be more costly to trade. In fact, the bid/ask trading costs can vary anywhere from .02% of the trade on the largest companies to more than 2% for the smallest companies.[25] This means that an investor must pay this expense on both the buy side and the sell side of the trade when they are moving stocks around.

## Commissions

The next cost we'll discuss is a category most of us are familiar with—commissions. Although you don't see the cost of commissions in the management fee of your mutual fund, the cost is very real. Whether they're discussed or not, mutual funds often pay significant commissions on trades taking place inside the fund.

Mutual funds are reluctant to give detailed information on these costs because it is not required and could put them at a competitive disadvantage. Publishing information that your competitors are not obligated to provide can cause problems when selling your product, but the good news is that you can find out what commissions you are being charged by requesting a document known as a *Statement of Additional Information.* It's a good idea to see what commissions you pay, but be aware that what you discover may surprise you. *The Wall Street Journal* had fund tracker Lipper Inc. study 2000 funds. Through their study, they found that brokerage commissions alone "can more than double the cost of owning fund shares."[26] These and other expenses are certainly news to most investors as evidenced by a study released in 2014. The study found that nearly half of investors thought they paid no expenses in their retirement accounts and another 19% thought they were less than .5%.[27]

Another cost of investing that few investors are aware of is the expense of soft dollar arrangements. Soft dollar arrangements use client commissions to buy research that helps managers make investment decisions. They allow managers to pay for research costs without giving up more of the management fee. It's also a good way to hide expenses from investors who don't look beyond visible management fees.

## Market Impact

One of the biggest expenses in the world of investing involved a concept called *market impact*. This term refers to the implicit cost of trading a large block of stock in a short amount of time. Anyone who has taken a basic economics class knows what happens when you try to sell a large quantity of something when there is little demand for it. The price, of course, will go down. Conversely, the price of an item in limited supply will go up when demand suddenly spikes. You've probably witnessed this phenomenon when a hot new car comes out. If the demand is higher than the supply, it is not unusual for the car to sell for far more than its sticker price.

The same process occurs in the stock market. If a mutual fund grows too large and is managing a great deal of client assets, any trading that the fund engages in can actually move stock prices against the fund. In other words, they will drive the price of stocks they are selling down and the price of stocks they are buying up. Market impact is a hidden cost of which investors are rarely aware.

Market impact is most significant in the area of small or thinly traded stocks. This is because these stocks aren't traded in high volumes every day. If a fund manager is trying to get rid of 500,000 shares of a stock on a given day, it may be difficult if that stock normally trades only 100,000 shares a day. The manager will be faced with tremendous pressure to drop the price in order to sell all of the shares.

Investment managers are well aware of these expenses and often try to reduce them by altering their trading activity. For example, fund managers may actually delay the purchase of a stock, or ease into it to avoid significantly driving up its price. They may actually scrap the purchase altogether if the price rises excessively. Although there is no real expense incurred by this activity, there is a cost to the investor. It is often referred to as an *implicit expense* or *lost opportunity cost*. Since stocks go up more than they go down, any delay in buying will likely result in lost returns to the investor.

These hidden expenses can also vary based on the size of the mutual fund. In an April 2016 Boston College white paper entitled "Mutual Fund Transaction

Costs," the authors point out that large fund companies can actually be at a disadvantage to smaller funds due to the scale of their assets and the size of the trades they often must execute.[28] Although many big mutual fund companies and investment firms enjoy large m arketing budgets, it pays to keep in mind that bigger isn't always better when it comes to investing.

## Reducing Expenses

One way to avoid these expenses is to avoid funds that trade stocks too frequently. This practice can be tricky, because some funds may trade a lot one year and very little the next. To find out which funds aren't engaging in excess trading in the most recent reporting period, look at the fund's *turnover ratio*. This ratio can be easily found in the fund's prospectus. A turnover ratio of 90% means that 90% of the fund's assets were sold during the preceding year. You may also want to look at the fund's objective in the prospectus to discover the fund manager's philosophy regarding stock trading. If you read that the fund manager's objective is to find underpriced stocks or to get rid of overvalued stocks, it's a sure sign that the fund will be subject to frequent trading. It is better and safer to find funds where the objective is to simply match market returns.

An acceptable amount of turnover can vary based on the asset class in which the fund is investing. In general, stock funds will have much lower turnover than bond funds. That is because bonds mature on a regular basis and must be replaced. When looking for a large U.S. stock fund, you must be more particular about the amount of turnover than you would in a small U.S. stock fund. The reason is that small companies grow and become medium-sized companies. As they move away from the intended asset class target (from small to medium-sized) we want and expect the fund manager to sell the stocks, take the gains, and invest in the upcoming small companies. The same is true in value mutual funds. In any case, it is rare for a fund to turnover by any more than 30% to 40% in any given year, and large growth funds are usually in the range of 10% and below.

Be aware that some funds may have low turnover ratios but still have a lot of trading activity. For example, a target-date fund, or funds that hold other mutual funds, may show a low turnover when reading the prospectus. In that case you have to dig deeper and look at the turnover inside the funds held by the fund. Who said this stuff was easy?

## Taxes and Turnover

Low turnover doesn't simply help keep upfront investor costs down. By keeping turnover low, there is also a benefit in the tax management of a portfolio. Each time stocks are traded in a mutual fund, taxable gains may be passed on to the fund's shareholders. As a rule, the less trading that takes place, the more money investors can keep for themselves.

One way to protect yourself is to make sure that your funds are tax managed if they are going to be held in a taxable account. A *tax-managed fund* may keep taxes low by engaging in several different strategies:

1. Low turnover, as previously discussed

2. Off-setting capital gains with capital losses

3. Holding stocks that historically keep taxable dividends low

4. Selling higher basis stocks in order to avoid selling lower basis stocks.

5. Rebalancing portfolios with cash flows versus selling over- weighted assets and buying underweighted segments.

We've now covered all four major myths of investing and how they are used in an attempt to entice more investor money into the market. First we discussed **Stock Picking** and how it simply doesn't work. There is no magical stock picking ability, and chances are, you or your broker will not stumble upon the next Amazon through some lucky guessing. Then we talked about **Market Timing** and the dangers of playing the market according to this risky and ultimately unsuccessful investment model. Next we dispelled the myth that using the **Past Performance** of a fund is useful in selecting the right fund for you. And finally, we have just finished discussing the dramatic effect that **Expenses** can have on your portfolio, and that they do really matter.

Ultimately, to have sustainable, long-term success as an investor, it is imperative to learn about and be wary of these myths. The media and many fund managers and companies want you to believe these myths. Why? Because they want more of your money. Their concern is not your return, and the result of this misplaced concern is an elaborate production of smoke and mirrors to make you believe that they know how to make the most of your money. There are good funds and wise investments out there, and the **confident** investor is the educated investor.

Now we'll shift gears into a topic that is both the reason that many invest, and simultaneously the reason that others choose *not* to invest in the market. It is the concept of risk.

## Summary

- The final myth is the idea that expenses don't matter.

- Every time a fund manager buys and sells a stock, they must pay for that trade. And each expense—no matter how big or small—can have a dramatic effect on the returns.

- Although you don't see the cost of commissions on internal trades disclosed in the management fee of your mutual fund, the cost is very real.

- Brokerage commissions alone can more than double the cost of owning fund shares.

- Market impact refers to the implicit cost of trading a large block of stock in a short amount of time. Market impact is most significant in the area of small or thinly traded stocks.

- Sometimes although there may be no real "expense" incurred by investment activity, there can still be a cost to the investor. It is often referred to as an implicit expense or lost opportunity cost.

- To find out which funds aren't engaging in excess trading in the most recent reporting period, look at the fund's turnover ratio, which is found in the fund's prospectus.

- An acceptable amount of turnover can vary based on the asset class in which the fund is investing. By keeping turnover low, there is also a benefit in the tax management of a portfolio.

- One way to protect yourself is to make sure that your funds are tax-managed if they are going to be held in a taxable account. A tax-managed fund may keep taxes low by engaging in any number of strategies including 1) Low- turnover 2) Off-setting capital gains with capital losses 3) Holding stocks that historically keep taxable dividends low 4) Selling higher basis stocks in order to avoid selling lower basis stocks. 5) Rebalancing with cash flows.

## Quick Quiz

1. What is the fourth myth of investing?

2. What is the expense ratio or management fee?

3. True or False: Because more effort is needed to fill orders (and therefore more risk is incurred), large companies tend to be more costly to trade.

4. Is it required that investment companies and fund managers provide detailed information on commissions on internal trades to investors? And why are companies reluctant to do so?

5. What is a soft dollar arrangement and how are soft dollars used?

6. If a mutual fund grows too large and is managing a great deal of client assets, any trading that the fund engages in can actually move stock prices against the fund. In other words, they will drive the price of stocks they are selling down and the price of stocks they are buying up. What is this phenomenon called?

7. What is one of the best ways to avoid implicit and unnecessary fees and costs?

8. What is an effective way to determine which funds aren't engaging in excess trading?

9. If you read in the prospectus that a fund manager's objective is to find____stocks or to get rid of____stocks, it's a sure sign that the fund will be subject to frequent trading.

10. What strategies can a fund use to keep taxes low?

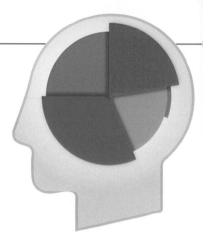

# Measuring Risk

**A**t this point in the book, it is important to delve into the concept of risk in investing. When most people hear the word "risk," they envision losing all of their money, and quite often, the word can even evoke fear in investors. However, the term *risk* can and should be used more broadly than that. In previous chapters, we discussed the different types of risk that investors face investing in the stock and bond markets, so now it is important to grasp the concept of how to measure this risk.

Too often, investment advisors talk about risk in the most generic terms. However, without the ability to specifically measure risk, we can't make well-informed decisions about the best way to design our portfolio. Our odds of having a successful investing experience can literally depend on making sure that we don't take too much or too little risk. If we don't take enough market risk, we can lose ground to inflation. If we take too much market risk, we run the risk of the market being down just when we need the money. There are two sides to the coin of risk—*downside risk* and *upside risk.* Everyone loves the upside variety, but it is downside risk that makes people nervous. However, you can't have one without the other. The key is to have a tool to measure the amount of upside and downside risk we are likely to face as investors, and that tool is standard deviation.

## Standard Deviation

*Standard deviation* is a measure that tells us how much our portfolio is likely to deviate or vary from the expected return if it has a normal distribution of returns. If I have a portfolio with an expected return of 10% and a standard deviation of 17, then approximately 68% (or a little over two-thirds) of my returns would historically fall between 27% and negative 7% (which is 10 plus or minus 17). The other (a little less than) one-third of returns we would expect to be above 27% or below negative 7% with 95% of returns falling between

44% and negative 24% (10 plus or minus 2 times 17). As you can see, the lower the standard deviation number is, the less the portfolio deviates from the average.

Imagine a child walking up a set of stairs with a yo-yo. The general trend of the yo-yo will be up as the child climbs the stairs, but because the yo-yo itself is going up and down, there will be times when the toy's altitude will go down despite the child's climb. If the string is short, then the downward movements will be small. Think of that short string as a low standard deviation; conversely, if the string is long, it has a high standard deviation.

You may have noticed that I mentioned historical returns as I described standard deviation. As you know, there are no guarantees about the future. Things can always happen that have never occurred before. Standard deviation just gives us a tool to shed light on possible outcomes in the future based on the past. It is for this reason that we like to have as much data as we can for the longest period of time possible when determining the best mix for our portfolio. Most of the data on stocks goes back to the 1920s. Since that period, we have seen great changes—both good and bad—that have given us a glimpse of how the market reacts to various scenarios.

## Risk and the Probability of Success

The measurement of risk is a primary tool used in a process called *probability analysis*, or a *Monte Carlo simulation*. The idea behind such a simulation is that people like to know their odds of having a successful outcome with their chosen investment strategy. If an investor realizes beforehand that the strategy he is using has little odds of success, then he may be inclined to look for other strategies that may lead to a better chance of success.

The major problem that Monte Carlo simulations solve is that returns in the market are unpredictable; therefore, linear returns projections don't give us a realistic picture of what is likely to happen with our investments over time. In other words, even though an asset category may have a long history of increasing an average of 10% per year, that doesn't mean it really goes up 10% every year. However, linear projections make that unrealistic assumption. They assume your returns over a five-year period will be: 10%, 10%, 10%, 10%, and 10% (scenario 1 as represented by the dotted line on this page), but what happens if your returns are: -15%, -10%, 12%, 34%, and 40% (scenario 2 as represented by the thick purple line on this page)? The average return is approximately the same, but the outcome can be quite different. The opposite is also true; if the high returns occur in the early years, then we could have a completely different outcome depending on our investment cash flows (scenario 3 as represented by the thin blue line on this page).

If you pull out a calculator, you will notice that $100 in all three scenarios grows to approximately $161. The difference becomes apparent when you start to deposit or withdraw money. If you were accumulating money for retirement, you would have the best result with the negative returns occurring first. For example, if you put $10,000 per year away at the beginning of each year, your deposits would be worth a little over $88,000.

However, if the negative returns occurred last, your accumulation would be less than $53,000. The linear method that most people use would have projected an accumulation between those two numbers—around $67,000.

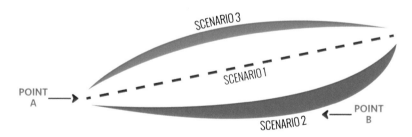

Why are the outcomes so different? The order of the returns an investor experiences can be more important than their average return, and this graph shows why.

If I am accumulating money for retirement, I won't have the bulk of my money at point "A." That is because I have just started the process. I will have more money at point "B," which is the amount after I've made a few deposits. If you look at the bold purple line, which represents negative returns in the beginning, you can see how the high returns that occur when I have the most money can really drive accumulation up.

If I am distributing money in retirement, the bold line scenario can lead to problems. That is because I have the most money at point "A." When the market drops, I will be forced to sell more shares of my investment to make sure I get the income I need. This is sometimes referred to as *reverse dollar cost averaging*. Dollar cost averaging can give us lower average share costs when we are accumulating money, which is a positive benefit. In other words, if I am putting a set amount of money away each year, every time the market drops I will purchase more shares of my investment. If it goes up, I will purchase fewer shares. That means I will buy more "low" and less "high."

This process works against me, though, if I am pulling money out, which is why it is so important to know the amount of risk of your portfolio. Again, the idea is to balance market risk with inflation risk and not take too much of either variety, and this is where Monte Carl analysis comes in. By projecting different return scenarios and how the investor may be affected by each, you can determine if you should be saving more money or reducing the amount of your distribution in retirement.

## How Monte Carlo Works

In a Monte Carlo analysis, the investor inputs data on their financial situation, and a computer model outputs the range of outcomes that are possible based on that data. The data that is typically needed for this calculation include: Current accumulation, additional deposits anticipated, expected return, inflation rate expected, years to retirement, and amount of distribution in retirement. The computer takes the returns and randomizes them using the standard deviation data provided. For instance, if the expected return is 10% and the standard deviation is 17 (as in our above example), then approximately two-thirds of the returns generated by the software will be between 10% plus or minus 17 (27% to negative 7%), and another approximately 27% will be between 44% and 27%, or negative 7% and negative 24%. 5% of returns will be above 44% or below negative 24%. Thank God for computers.

By running hundreds of iterations (or return scenarios) on a computer, you can get a better feel for possible outcomes that are likely based on the data provided. As you can imagine, an investor who doesn't know the possible range of returns can't very well prepare for a scenario where the order of returns don't fall in their favor.

## Using Monte Carlo Software

Simulation software is readily available on the Internet, but a word of caution is in order. The software's outputs are only as good as the inputs used. As they say in the computer business, "garbage in, garbage out." You must know the expected returns of your portfolio, the expected risk measure (standard deviation), and use a reasonable inflation rate in your calculations. Often, this is a project that is best left to an experienced advisor. Well-informed advisors should have access to the most sophisticated types of software that allow them to determine the expected rates of returns on various portfolio designs as well as their historical risks and inflation assumptions.

This software and calculating the standard deviation of a portfolio can help you make more informed decisions, but there is far more to the process than a few calculations. In the next chapter, we'll go into greater detail of the foundations of successful fund and portfolio selection.

## Summary

- Without the ability to specifically measure risk, we can't make well-informed decisions about the best way to design our portfolio.

- There are two sides to the coin of risk—downside risk and upside risk. The key is to have a tool to measure both types of risk we are likely to face as investors—and that tool is standard deviation.

- Standard deviation is a measure that tells us how much our portfolio is likely to deviate or vary from the expected return.

- The measurement of risk is a primary tool used in a process called probability analysis, or Monte Carlo simulations.

- The major problem that Monte Carlo simulations solve is that returns in the market are unpredictable. The simulations help an investor determine their odds of success in meeting their goals where linear projections may give a false sense of security.

- Monte Carlo analysis also helps by projecting different return scenarios and how each may affect the investor, which helps determine if you should be saving more money or reducing the amount of your distribution.

- In order to trust the results of simulation, you must know the expected returns of your portfolio, the expected risk measure (standard deviation), and use a reasonable inflation rate in your calculations. Due to the complexity of the calculations, this is often a project that is best left to an experienced advisor.

## Quick Quiz

1. What tool helps measure both upside and downside risk?

2. What does standard deviation tell us in relation to a portfolio?

3. Things can always happen that have never occurred before. Standard deviation just gives us a tool to shed light on possible outcomes in the _____ based on the _____.

4. The measurement of risk is a primary tool used in a process called probability analysis. What is another name for this process?

5. True or False: The major problem that linear simulations solve is that returns in the market are unpredictable.

6. How does Monte Carlo simulation help determine the most efficient amount of money to contribute to your retirement fund?

7. What data is typically needed for a Monte Carlo calculation?

8. True or False: Monte Carlo simulation software is easy to use for beginning investors.

## CHAPTER ELEVEN

# FOUNDATIONSFOR INVESTMENT SUCCESS

## PART ONE

# Foundations for Investment Success, Part 1

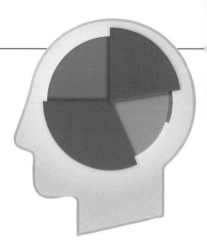

**I**|**f you construct a building** with a strong foundation based on an organized plan of assembly, your building won't just last; it will be sturdy and reliable. Just as a strong foundation is critical to the longevity of a building, a strong foundation in the logic behind your investment strategy is also of great importance. Investors who don't know *why* they are doing what they are doing won't do it for very long—and it definitely won't be done well. The lack of discipline and an absence of proper planning are the biggest causes of failure amongst investors. The best way to get people to stay the course is to make sure you know the *why* behind your portfolio design.

In this chapter, we'll look at various asset classes and begin to discuss why proper asset allocation into a mix of these classes is essential for building a strong investment foundation. Then we will continue our discussion of building a proper foundation for long-term success in chapter twelve as we cover the practical application of asset classes and their well-planned allocation.

## Evidence of the Problem

Experts conducted a number of studies to discover why investors do so poorly even though the stock market delivered stellar returns throughout its history. One study previously referenced in this book is from Dalbar Research in Boston. Dalbar has been examining investors' decisions to buy, hold, and sell mutual funds since 1987, and they found that investor behavior is the biggest deterrent to their success. Even though the S&P 500 delivered returns in excess of 10% from 1987 to 2016, according to their research, the average investor earned only 3.98% in the stock market.

*What are investors doing wrong?* The biggest problem stems from not having any confidence in their investment strategies. The average investor has little patience when investing in the stock market. According to Dalbar, investors only hold on to mutual funds for an average of approximately 3.8 years. Several other studies verify this behavioral shortcoming as well. The following graph shows how investors respond to market movements.[29]

## Net New Cash Flows To Equity Mutual Funds

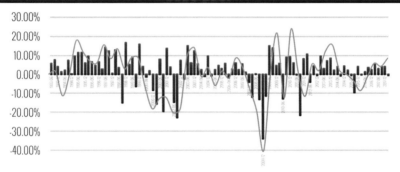

*Data from Morningstar and dimensional returns software

The blue bars represent money going in and out of the market. The green line represents the market return. As you can see, when the market is up, more money flows in, but when the market is down, money flows out. It's a simple case of selling low and buying high. It is not too difficult to keep an investor disciplined when markets are increasing and everything is going well, but it is next to impossible when bad news is everywhere and stocks fall. *Always remember that your choice to sell stocks is a prediction that the future will look like the immediate past.*

## The Big Secret Revealed

What if you could find out what really drives the returns you are likely to experience as an investor? Your chances of being successful would increase dramatically. Well, I have good news; such information does exist. In 1986, three academics named Gary P. Brinson, L. Randolph Hood, and Gilbert L. Beebower published a study of ninety-one pension plans and the factors that determined their performance over a ten-year period from 1974 to 1983.[30] The authors of the study replaced the pension funds' stock, bond, and cash selections with simple indexes, and by doing so, they achieved performance that was as good as—if not better than—the professional pension managers. They repeated the study in 1991 with similar results.

The studies found that three factors were primarily responsible for the performance they witnessed in the world of pensions: 1) stock selection 2) market timing and 3) asset allocation. This study is highly useful because it gives us a glimpse into the investment strategies of some of the highest paid, brightest, and best informed investors out there—pension fund managers—who are naturally regulated by the fact that they have a fiduciary responsibility to the corporations whose pensions they manage.

## The Big Picture

While all three factors play a role in portfolio performance, the vast majority of performance is driven by only one factor—the asset mix. As you can see from the graph below, the percentage of performance that is affected by asset allocation towers over the other two variables.[31]

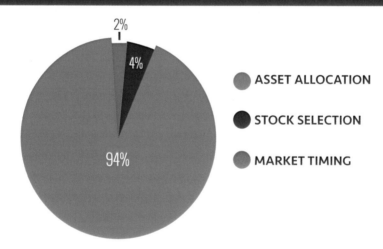

**DETERMINANTS OF PORTFOLIO PERFORMANCE**

2%
4%
94%

● ASSET ALLOCATION

● STOCK SELECTION

● MARKET TIMING

As we've already discussed, attempts at timing the market and selecting the best stocks drive investment performance down more often than not. Asset allocation is the most important aspect to focus on as an investor. Since that is the most crucial factor, let's spend some time looking at asset classes and how to define them.

## Asset Classes

To use an admittedly corny example, let's say that asset classes are like vehicles that are to be used in a big race to which everyone is invited. Imagine seeing a full-page ad in your local newspaper announcing a huge cross-country race next week. You are invited to attend and bring the vehicle of your choice, but there's only one stipulation. You won't be told what the racecourse will look like. In fact, you won't know anything at all until the race starts.

On race day, the starting line is full of different types of vehicles. One person brought a snowmobile, another showed up with a motorcycle, another rode in on a dune buggy, and yet another is driving a racecar. At the starting line there is a huge veil that makes it impossible to see the racecourse. As the starting gun fires, the veil lifts and the course is revealed. The road is snow-covered for the first patch of the race, so it is clear that the person who brought the snowmobile has the advantage in the first leg of the race. However, this doesn't mean that his advantage will last for long. The next patch of terrain may be sand. In that case, the dune buggy holds the advantage.

This is much like the world of asset class investing. We only have a clouded view of what economic terrain lies ahead. In the late 1980s, the terrain was best for international companies. In the early 1990s, the conditions were ripe for small U.S. companies. In the late 1990s, all lights were green for U.S. large stocks. The early 2000s were great for value stocks, international small and emerging markets. I remember entering the financial industry in 1989 when I was told by the older, more experienced, investment advisors in my office that I should just put my clients in international stocks. The assumption that they made was that international would continue to lead the field. This turned out to be very bad advice. Luckily, I didn't take it. The bottom line is that we don't know what the future has in store, but we do know this—it will be unpredictable.

## Broad Diversification

As you have seen, the "vehicles" in the previous example stand for different asset classes in the investing process. These asset classes have unique characteristics that cause them to behave differently depending on what is going on in the economy. It is important to have exposure to many of these investment areas rather than betting everything on one or two of them. Narrowly investing your money in a few select areas is like betting everything on the motorcycle in the preceding example. It probably would have wiped out early in the race on the snow-covered ground. That is why it's much safer to place your bets across all of the vehicles.

## Asset Class Examples

The six different asset classes we will cover in the next few sections are:

1. Treasury Bills

2. Treasury Bonds

3. Large U.S. Stocks

4. Large International Stocks

5. Small U.S. Stocks

6. Small International Stocks

To begin, let's look at the historical returns of the six asset classes as they compare to one another. As you can see from the following chart (whose information dates back to 1973), all of the stock categories delivered respectable returns.[32]

Now, let's take look at six basic asset categories and how they differ over a forty-five year period ending in 2017. As we delve into each category, we'll discuss the risks and benefits of each.

| 1973-2017 | | | | | | | |
|---|---|---|---|---|---|---|---|
| | US Inflation Rate | US Treasury Bills | Long Term US Govt Bonds | US Large Stocks | US Small Stocks | Intl Large Stocks | Intl Small Stocks |
| Annual Return | N/A | 4.74% | 8.19% | 10.42% | 12.39% | 9.10% | 13.24% |
| Annual Inflation Rate | 4.00% | 4.00% | 4.00% | 4.00% | 4.00% | 4.00% | 4.00% |
| Real Return | N/A | 0.74% | 4.19% | 6.42% | 8.39% | 5.10% | 9.24% |
| Negative Years | 0 | 0 | 12 | 9 | 13 | 13 | 12 |
| Positive Years | 45 | 45 | 33 | 36 | 32 | 32 | 33 |
| Total Years | 45 | 45 | 45 | 45 | 45 | 45 | 45 |
| Standard Deviation | N/A | 1.00% | 10.75% | 15.13% | 20.99% | 17.04% | 17.64% |
| **WORST PERFORMANCE YEAR** | | | | | | | |
| Year | 1979 | 2014 | 2009 | 2008 | 2008 | 2008 | 2008 |
| Loss % | 13.29% | 0.02% | -14.90% | -37.00% | -38.72% | -43.06% | -46.46% |
| **BEST PERFORMANCE YEAR** | | | | | | | |
| Year | 2008 | 1981 | 1982 | 1995 | 1975 | 1986 | 1977 |
| Gain % | 0.09% | 14.71% | 40.36% | 37.58% | 63.92% | 69.94% | 74.08% |

## Treasury Bills

The first asset category is Treasury bills. When the government borrows money for less than one year they issue Treasury bills (also known as T-bills). T-bills are the standard for low-risk investing in the industry because they mature in less than one year, so there is little interest rate risk. There is also minimal risk of default, because the government always has the option to increase taxes or print money to repay its bills.

Because there is little risk of losing money in T-bills, there is also little "risk" that you will make much money. In fact, over the past eighty years, T-bills only returned approximately .5 percent after inflation (as measured by the consumer price index). At that rate, it takes over one hundred years for money to double. Most of us don't have that long to wait. The rate of return for the last forty -five years ending in 2017 is .74 percent after inflation. Thus, that is the biggest problem with safe fixed income investments; they do little to protect investors from the depreciation of the purchasing power of the dollar.

What fixed income investments do well, however, is protect the principal of our investments from short-term declines. This makes them useful for emergency funds and short-term goals. They are also useful in our portfolio as the one vehicle that will always go up. In the last thirty-five years, T-bills have never had a negative year. The usefulness of this trait will become apparent when we talk about the benefits of portfolio rebalancing in the next chapter.

## Treasury Bonds

The next basic asset category is Treasury bonds. Treasury bonds (or T-bonds) are issued when the government borrows money for ten to thirty years. Because an investor is locking up money for a greater amount of time with T-bonds, they are prone to interest rate risk. If interest rates go up, bond prices go down to compensate. In our forty-five year period example, T-bonds delivered negative returns in twelve of those years. The biggest decline occurred in 1999 when T-bonds lost almost fifteen percent.

Since the borrower is the same entity with T-bills and T-bonds, we have a good laboratory to view the risk/return trade-off. Since there is more risk with T- bonds, we expect that the rate of return should be higher, and in fact, this is exactly what we observe. T-bonds outpaced inflation by 4.19 percent over our forty-five year period. It is the same borrower, but they must pay more interest in order to get investors to take the increased risk.

One of the helpful aspects of T-bonds is that they have a tendency to move in dissimilar fashion with the stock market. Treasuries often rally when the market goes down, because despite the potential short-term volatility of T-Bonds, investors are assured of getting their money back when the bond matures. This dissimilar price movement helps dampen the volatility of portfolios.

## Large U.S. Stocks

This asset class needs almost no explanation. Large U.S. stocks are a favorite among American investors. After all, these are the companies we read about every day in the news. Large U.S. stocks have a long history of fairly consistent returns over long periods of time. From 1973 to 2017, large U.S. stocks averaged about a 10.42 percent per year return. That translates to over 6.42 percent return per year after inflation. In exchange for higher returns, though, investors must put up with significantly higher volatility. To illustrate, large U.S. stocks dropped thirty- seven percent in value in 2008 and rose in value over thirty-seven percent in 1995.[33] U.S stocks may sometimes have some heavy volatility, but their returns over inflation for the past thirty-five years make them a useful part of almost any portfolio.

## Large International Stocks

Similar to large U.S. stocks, large international stocks provided approximately eleven percent return from 1973 to 2017. The *returns* are similar because the *risks* are similar. Large international company returns range from almost seventy percent on the high end to a little over -43 percent on the low end.[34] Many large international firms operate all over the world, just as big U.S. companies operate multi- nationally. They tend to be well-run companies that vigorously compete with one another. According to Morningstar, as of the end of 2016, approximately forty-six percent of the value of publicly traded companies is located outside the United States (See the chart entitled Stock Market Capitalization).[35] Many of these companies are household names such as: Nestle, Sony, Bridgestone, Toyota, BP, Roche, and Adidas.

Despite the similar risks and returns of large international and large U.S. stock, these large international companies don't always move in tandem with large U.S. companies. One of the reasons is that significant amounts of man-ufacturing activity take place outside of the U.S., just as the U.S. begins to lean more and more toward being a service economy. Another reason has to do with exchange rate risk between the dollar and other currencies. If the dollar drops in value verses other currencies, international stocks increase in value in America. That is because it takes more dollars to buy those interna-tional entities. The opposite is also true. These factors add to the allure of holding international stocks, because they help diversify by providing more dissimilar price movement within the portfolio, and that tends to reduce risk.

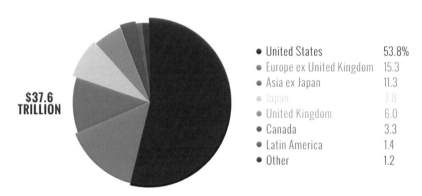

**WORLD STOCK MARKET CAPITALIZATION**
Year-End 2016

$37.6 TRILLION

| | |
|---|---|
| • United States | 53.8% |
| • Europe ex United Kingdom | 15.3 |
| • Asia ex Japan | 11.3 |
| • Japan | 7.8 |
| • United Kingdom | 6.0 |
| • Canada | 3.3 |
| • Latin America | 1.4 |
| • Other | 1.2 |

Capitalization calculated at year-end 2016. Total market capitalization is $37.6 trillion. Estimates are not guaranteed.
© Morningstar. All Rights Reserved.

## Small U.S. Stocks

Small U.S. stocks have provided even greater returns than large U.S. stocks throughout time. From 1973 to 2017, they had an annualized return of 12.4 percent. Small companies tend to move differently from large U.S. compa-nies because they are more regional in focus. Many small U.S. companies never venture outside the United States when searching for customers. In addition, small companies can often implement new technology much faster than their large company counterparts. They often change direction faster as well, because there is commonly less bureaucracy.

With all of that said, there can also be more volatility with small stocks. Where U.S. large companies dropped twenty-six percent in 1974, small U.S. companies went down over thirty-eight percent the year before. They have also gone through greater upside volatility as well. In 2003, small U.S. stocks shot up over seventy-eight percent.[36] As with the other asset classes mentioned, small companies can serve to dampen volatility, because they don't usually move in lock step with other areas of the market. For instance, in 1998 small U.S. stock went down eight percent while large U.S. companies went up over twenty-eight percent. In 2001, the reverse was true. Large companies dropped almost twelve percent, but small companies jumped almost thirty-four percent.

## Small International Stocks

Just as small U.S. companies tend to outpace large U.S. companies over time, small international companies can have higher returns than their large international counterparts. From 1973 to 2017, international small companies averaged over thirteen percent returns verses around nine percent for large international. The lowest return for the category occurred in 2008 when these stocks went down over forty-six percent in value. Conversely, they jumped over seventy-four percent in 1977. American investors are often reluctant to add this group of stocks to their portfolios, because they represent a group of stocks that many of us have never even heard of (nor can we pronounce the names of many of them), and because it seems that owning them would drastically increase the risk of our portfolios. However, research in portfolio design actually shows that we can reduce risk by adding small international stocks to the asset allocation mix.

Now that we know the basics about each asset category, and as mentioned earlier, the only predictable thing about which asset category will do well is that the answer is unpredictable. That is why it is imperative to *spread the wealth* across multiple assets. In the next chapter, we'll use the information about each category to show you how to make proper asset allocations that build a strong investment foundation.

## Summary

- The lack of discipline and planning are the biggest causes of failure amongst investors; so the best way to stay the course is to know the why behind your portfolio design.

- Three factors are primarily responsible for portfolio performance: 1) Stock selection 2) Market timing 3) Asset allocation, with the vast majority of performance driven by only one factor—the asset mix.

- The six basic asset classes are: 1) Treasury bills 2) Treasury bonds 3) Large U.S. stocks 4) Large international stocks 5) Small U.S. stocks 6) Small international stocks.

- When the government borrows money for less than one year, they issue Treasury bills (also known as T-bills), which are the standard for low-risk investing in the industry. They are needed to protect the principal of our investments from short-term declines.

- Treasury bonds (or T-bonds) are issued when the government borrows money for ten to thirty years, and they have a tendency to move in dissimilar fashion with the stock market.

- Large U.S. stocks are a favorite among American investors and have a long history of fairly consistent returns over long periods of time.

- Large international stocks have similar risks and returns to large U.S. stocks, but they don't always move in tandem with large U.S. companies.

- Small U.S. stocks have provided even greater returns than large U.S. stocks throughout time, but there can also be more volatility with small stocks.

- Small international companies can have higher returns than their large international counterparts. Research in portfolio design actually shows that we can reduce risk by adding small international stocks to the asset allocation mix.

## Quick Quiz

1. What are the primary causes of failure amongst investors?

2. What is the best way to feel confident enough to stay in your investments no matter the current economic climate?

3. The biggest problem in investing stems from not having any confidence in your own _____ _____.

4. True or False: Always remember that your choice to sell stocks is a prediction that the future will look like the immediate past.

5. What is the most important factor in portfolio performance?

6. Name the six main asset classes.

7. Which asset class has the lowest risk and what is its main purpose?

8. Because an investor is locking up money for a greater amount of time with T-bonds, they are prone to _____ _____ risk.

9. When it comes to stocks, in exchange for higher potential returns, what must investors contend with?

10. True or False: Because of their many similarities, large international stocks and large U.S. stocks always move in tandem with each other.

11. What are a few advantages of owning small U.S. stocks?

12. Despite the commonly held belief of the average investor that international stocks are too risky, what is true of small international stocks?

"Money is like manure.
You have to spread it
around or it smells."

-J. Paul Getty

CHAPTER TWELVE

# FOUNDATIONS FOR INVESTMENT SUCCESS

PART TWO

# Foundations for Investment Success, Part 2

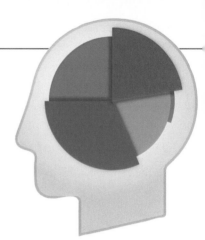

**W**e've now seen that the lack of investor confidence places some serious obstacles in the way of portfolio success. So how do we remedy that? And what is the only lasting way to gain confidence in your investment decisions? The answer is simple: Become educated. Many of the nervous, hesitant investors are that way simply because they lack basic knowledge of the concepts and principles of investing, thus becoming easy targets for investing myths, clever fund marketing, and Wall Street scare tactics. And by now you know that *education* is what this book is all about.

In the previous chapter, we began our discussion of the foundations of investment success, but we only laid the first few bricks. We can't build a lasting foundation without knowing the *how* behind concepts and terminology. Without the *how*, they're all just of meaningless words. Now we'll take the asset categories and show that proper asset allocation is not gut feelings and guesswork. There is a science to it. Is it an exact science? No. The proven theories in place can help give you real direction, and, ultimately, provide you with the confidence you need to tune out the Wall Street marketing machine and invest without fear.

## A "Nobel" Calling

Many of the concepts used in this book resulted in two Nobel Prizes in Economics. *No, I didn't win the Nobel Prize.* In 1990 University of Chicago professor Harry Markowitz, along with Merton Miller and William Sharpe, won the first; and In 2013 Eugene Fama, also of Chicago, won another. Markowitz' work actually began nearly forty years earlier when he decided to apply mathematics to the study of the stock market. His brainchild from the research is called the *Efficient Frontier*, which is graph representing the portfolio mixes with the highest expected return within an investor's given level of risk.

I often hear investment advisors say that they devise every portfolio differently, because every investor is different. In the Nobel Prize-winning world of Markowitz, that idea is nonsense. Investors basically want as much return as they can get for the select amount of volatility they can stomach, so they really aren't all that different. Here is a graphic representation of the Efficient Frontier:[37]

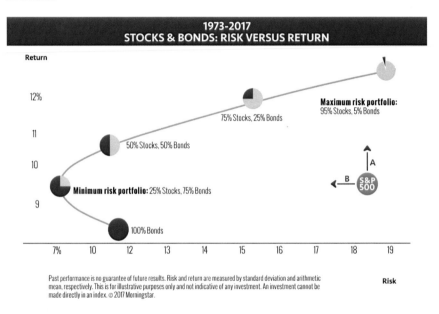

**1973-2017**
**STOCKS & BONDS: RISK VERSUS RETURN**

Return

12%

11

10

9

7%   10   12   13   14   15   16   17   18   19

75% Stocks, 25% Bonds

50% Stocks, 50% Bonds

Minimum risk portfolio: 25% Stocks, 75% Bonds

100% Bonds

Maximum risk portfolio:
95% Stocks, 5% Bonds

A

B   S&P 500

Past performance is no guarantee of future results. Risk and return are measured by standard deviation and arithmetic mean, respectively. This is for illustrative purposes only and not indicative of any investment. An investment cannot be made directly in an index. © 2017 Morningstar.

Risk

To explain this graph and the concept of the Efficient Frontier, let's say that an investor put all of his money into a fund that tracked the S&P 500 index. Markowitz contended that an investor could diversify the portfolio more broadly and pick up greater expected return for the risk taken (represented by arrow A). Alternatively, if the investor is not comfortable with the risk of owning the S&P 500 stocks, he could reallocate his mix and pick up a similar expected return, but with a fraction of the risk (represented by arrow B).

## The How Behind the Theory

The Efficient Frontier is based on an idea to which I have alluded; that is, the different asset classes move in dissimilar fashion with one another. Therefore, putting them together in a portfolio causes the whole to be less risky than the parts. In a perfect world, it may look like this:[38]

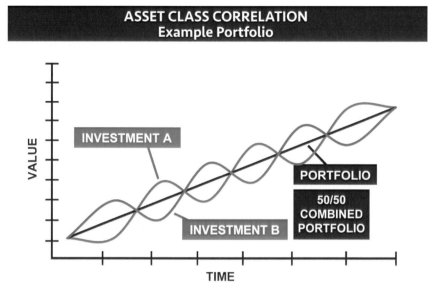

According to our perfect scenario, when one investment *zigs*, the other *zags*. Of course, this isn't always possible. If it were, we could create extremely high- returning portfolios with no risk, and it would make the use of CDs obsolete. The best we can hope for is to have the asset classes move differently enough to reduce the risk we experience. This is actually what tends to happen with portfolios designed in this manner. The reason is that portfolios are brought back to their target allocations on a regular basis. In English, this means that the above portfolio would be reallocated back to a 50/50 mix anytime it got too far out of balance. If investment A does poorly, but investment B does well, the fund manager would sell some of B and buy more of A. It is simply a matter of making sure your portfolio mix doesn't change drastically. It must remain true to your original intentions.

That idea may sound like a heresy, because most people are driven to sell the losers in their portfolios and buy more of the winners, but remember the golden rule of investing (and no, it's not, "Whoever has the gold rules"): Buy low and sell high. This may appear to be market timing, but it isn't, as long as it is done on a disciplined basis and not in response to our feelings about what we think may happen in the future.

As an example of how this works, look at the time period from 1988 to 2002. Large U.S. stocks and small U.S. stocks had the same exact return of

11.5% during that time period. A hypothetical investment of $50,000 in a non-taxable portfolio would have grown to $255,000 in either area of the market. Investing in both would have yielded $510,000. If you had put them together, however, and rebalanced annually, the new portfolio would have grown to approximately $543,000. That is a  difference  of  $33,000.[39] As a  side benefit, the new portfolio as a whole was less volatile (as measured by standard deviation) than the parts.

## The Rebalancing Act

Rebalancing your portfolio isn't just something you do annually no matter what. In fact, I don't typically recommend rebalancing your allocation unless your portfolio is deviating from your target percentages by 25% or more. In other words, if you have two different asset categories that should each be taking up 10% of your portfolio, it is not necessary to rebalance unless one of them is now at 12.5% or 7.5% (25% of 10% is 2.5%).

Another way to rebalance that I talked about in a previous chapter, is to make sure that money you add to the portfolio goes into the areas that are under-represented. Of course, you should do the opposite when pulling money out by withdrawing it from the areas that are overrepresented. Rebalancing may have to be tailored for your tax circumstances as well. If the rebalance will trigger unwanted taxes, then it may be best to wait for a more opportune time. As you can see, this is not for the faint of heart and may be best left to professionals.

## The Three Factor Model

What else explains the higher return we may expect from more diversified portfolios? One of the most important discoveries in modern investment research is a concept called the *Fama-French Three Factor Model* developed by Eugene Fama (Nobel Prize 2013) and Kenneth French. Their model explains three factors responsible for approximately ninety-five percent of the levels of returns you can expect from a portfolio. By changing your exposure to these factors, you can change the expected return of the portfolio, which also alters the amount of risk. The three factors considered in the model are 1) Stocks vs. Bonds 2) Small Companies vs. Large Companies and 3) Value Stocks vs. Growth Stocks. A more recently determined fourth factor using company profitability (Novy-Marx) is also important but beyond the scope of this book.

## Stocks vs. Bonds

The first factor of the Three Factor Model is the comparison of stocks versus bonds, which is often referred to as the *market factor*. As you know, stocks tend to outperform bonds over the long run; however, stocks are obviously more risky. In fact, from 1926 until 2017, one-month treasury bills averaged 3.35 percent with a standard deviation of .88—both low risk and low return. Stocks during that time period (as measured by the S&P 500) had a return of 10.16 percent with a standard deviation of 18.67—both higher risk and higher return.

## Small Companies vs. Large Companies

Just as stocks tend to deliver higher returns over time, small companies tend to display higher returns than large companies. This return difference is also the result of the increased volatility of the small company asset category. Small companies tend to be less immune to economic fluctuations and are more prone to financial difficulty. From 1926 to 2017, small stocks delivered returns of 12.1 percent with a much higher standard deviation of 31.98.

You may be wondering how to define a small company. Well, much of the research about stock returns and the data used in this book comes from the University of Chicago Center for Research in Security Prices (CRSP®). They have a database that actually breaks the market up into tenths or deciles. For example, decile one includes the largest ten percent of companies listed on the New York Stock Exchange as well as all like-size companies on the other exchanges. The database defines small or micro-cap companies as belonging to deciles nine through ten, which are the smallest twenty percent of the companies in the CRSP database.

Since companies generally grow, you can see how this makes "small" a moving target. To keep it simple, when searching for small company stock, I generally look for funds that hold stocks whose average market capitalization is less than two billion.

## Value Stocks vs. Growth Stocks

The third factor of the Three Factor Model is the one that surprises most investors. It is based on the same logic as the previous two, but because of the indoctrination of investors at the hand of the investment industry, at first blush it doesn't seem to make sense. It states that value stocks tend to outperform growth stocks. In other words, distressed companies tend to have higher returns than strong and stable companies. Many are surprised by this because they believe that the financial advisor's job is to make sure we own nothing but great companies in our portfolios.

If you compare great companies to poorly run companies, great companies seem to win in every area of financial analysis. They often have better asset growth, equity growth, return on total capital, return on equity, and return on sales.[40] Despite this fact, investors receive much higher returns from these distressed stocks than from their healthy counterparts. The reason is largely because investors aren't willing to pay as much for each dollar of earnings that a distressed company generates; therefore, any improvement in the operation of the company can cause a big climb in the stock's price.

I use an analogy from the world of golf to make this point. It starts by asking the question, "Who is a better golfer—Tiger Woods or Paul Winkler?" Most of my clients, knowing that I don't golf anymore (or that I ever really did), quickly say "Tiger." Then I ask a second question. "Who has a better shot of knocking ten strokes off of his score?" Now the answer becomes "Paul." All I have to do is hire a golf instructor for about an hour to discover a few secrets to improve my game and my score, but Tiger has already honed his game to peak efficiency.

The same is true for well-run companies; they are doing many of the things that make a company great, and their stock prices already reflect this. It is the companies that are not well run that have all the room for improvement.

## Value Companies Defined

Determining whether a mutual fund is truly investing in value companies can become ridiculously complex. Even experienced financial professionals some-times have a hard time figuring out which funds are truly focused on value stocks as defined by the Fama-French research, especially when the factor of profitability is part of the mix.

There are a several ways to define value companies in the investing world, so it's not as easy as looking at the fund's name to determine if it is truly focused on buying value stocks. A mutual fund may be called the ABC Value Fund but not really own any value stocks by the Fama-French definition. One way to determine if this is the case is to look at the objective of the fund in the fund prospectus. You may see that the goal of the fund manager is to find mispriced stocks that are supposedly a "value" on the stock market. Many academics don't like the word "value" because it implies that the stock is selling for less than it is worth. As we discussed, the market already does a pretty good job of making sure pricing imperfections get eliminated; so big bargains aren't necessarily just sitting out there waiting for a better-informed investor to sniff them out.

Other definitions of value focus on statistical measures and key financial ratios. Three commonly used ratios to identify value are price to earnings, price to sales, and price to book. As you can see, all three ratios compare the company's current stock price to another important financial number. The Fama- French research used only one of those ratios to define value—price to book because the other two ratios don't have a stable denominator. In other words, the other two ratio's denominators—earnings and sales—may fluctuate quite a bit from one year to the next in a company, but a company's book value (assets minus liabilities) tends to be more stable over time. This can be important, because it would make no sense if stocks jumped in and out of the value category on a frequent basis. Companies don't move in and out of distress in a rapid manner.

Further, the Fama-French research defined value companies as those companies whose price to book fell into the bottom thirty percent of all companies listed on the New York Stock Exchange. (Technically, they used the inverse of the ratio in their research, book to market.) It makes sense if you think about it. A company that is selling at or near the value of its assets minus what it owes (its liabilities) must be in some distress or investors would place a higher value on it.

## Staying Above the Crowd

Unfortunately, there is no easy or foolproof system to select a great value fund in your 401(k) or other retirement plan using the information in this chapter. The ratios defining value stocks are moving targets, especially as the investing climate changes. More often than not, a 401(k) plan won't even have a fund that truly meets any of the criteria we just discussed.

So what do you do? For one, you can look at the selections called value and try to select the ones containing stocks with lower Price-to-Book ratios. You can also utilize a useful tool called the Morningstar® Style Box. The

Style Box attempts to classify mutual funds in nine different areas: Large growth, large blend (core), large value, mid-cap growth, mid-cap blend, mid-cap value, small growth, small blend, and small value. Although their definition of value varies slightly from the one used above, it can be helpful as a starting point for choosing funds for your mix.

Keep in mind that these guidelines are rough at best. It is often well worth the money to hire a well-educated, fee-only advisor to assist in making proper selections for your portfolio. I cannot overemphasize the importance of this point. A primary goal of this book is to help you gain a solid foundation of knowledge in investing; however, it is not meant to replace a qualified investment advisor.

The concept of asset allocation should help you breathe a big sigh of relief. You can ignore all the noise from the investing industry assured that your mix of assets takes priority over everything else. You can ignore all of the hype about which stocks to buy, when to get in the market, when to get out, and what the Fed is going to do next. The key idea is that you can set up your portfolio mix based on your goals and then just maintain the mix through rebalancing.

Using Fama and French's three factors is like finger painting; if you take yellow and blue and mix them, you know you'll get green. The more yellow you add, the lighter the resulting shade of green. Changing exposure to these three factors can increase or decrease the expected returns and risk of your portfolio depending on what you want to accomplish.

In the next chapter, we will cover some basic portfolio mixes as starting points for designing your portfolio.

## Summary

- The only lasting way to gain confidence in your investment decisions is to become educated.

- Harry Markowitz's Nobel Prize-winning research led the Efficient Frontier, a graph representing the portfolio mixes with the highest expected return within an investor's given level of risk.

- The method behind the Efficient Frontier is based on the idea that the different asset classes move in dissimilar fashion with one another, and putting them together in a portfolio causes the whole to be less risky than the parts.

- Typically, you should not rebalance your allocation unless your portfolio is deviating from your target percentages by twenty-five percent or more.

- The Fama-French Three Factor Model explains that there are three factors responsible for approximately ninety-five percent of the levels of returns you can expect from a portfolio.

- The three factors considered in the model are: 1) Stocks vs. bonds (also known as the market factor) 2) Small companies vs. large companies and 3) Value stocks vs. growth stocks.

- Small companies tend to display higher returns than large companies. This return difference is also the result of the increased volatility of the small company asset category.

- The third factor in the Three Factor Model says that value stocks tend to outperform growth stocks, meaning that distressed companies tend to have higher returns than strong and stable companies.

- The Fama-French Model uses only one ratio to define value—the price- to-book ratio.

- You can utilize a useful tool called the Morningstar Style Box to help determine asset allocation, a tool that attempts to classify mutual funds in nine different areas: Large growth, large blend, large value, mid-cap growth, mid-cap blend, mid-cap value, small growth, small blend, and small value.

## Quick Quiz

1. What is the only lasting way to gain confidence in your investment decisions?

2. You can't build a lasting foundation in investment knowledge without knowing the _____ behind concepts and terminology.

3. What is the Efficient Frontier?

4. What idea is the Efficient Frontier is based on?

5. Typically, you should not rebalance your allocation unless your portfolio is deviating from your target percentages by _____-_____ percent or more.

6. What does the Fama-French Three Factor Model help explain?

7. What are the three factors considered in the Three Factor Model?

8. What is the first factor, stocks vs. bonds, often called? And what does it mean?

9. Just as stocks tend to deliver higher returns over time, _____ _____ tend to display higher returns than large companies.

10. The third factor of the Three Factor Model says that value stocks tend to outperform growth stocks over time. In layman's terms, what does this mean?

11. It is important to remember that the market already does a pretty good job of making sure that pricing imperfections get eliminated; so big_____aren't necessarily just sitting out there waiting for a better-informed investor to stumble upon them.

12. What commonly used ratio does the Fama-French model use to define value?

13. What tool can investors use to compare mutual funds, and how does this tool work?

## CHAPTER THIRTEEN
# PORTFOLIO MIXES

# Portfolio Mixes

**F**or most investors, choosing a portfolio mix consists of picking mutual funds with the best track record. As we've seen, that is not a winning strategy, and it usually leads to poor performance in the end. This selection method is the *grocery store approach* to investing, like a shopper walking into the grocery store without a shopping list. At the store, the shopper walks up and down the isles randomly dropping things into the cart while thinking, "Mmm, the cookies look good… The potato chips look tasty… Well, the cupcakes seem…"

A better approach is to have a definite goal in mind and a shopping list that reflects that goal. For instance, if my goal is to bake a cake, I might have a shopping list with eggs, flour, sugar, and frosting on it. In the same way, you need a shopping list for your investment portfolio. Just as you need a goal before you go grocery shopping, you also need a goal before you choose your investments.

## Setting Your Goal

The primary way to set a goal that leads to creating the proper investment mix involves choosing a time horizon. In other words, you must first determine how long you have until you need your money back. Other considerations in the process may involve the amount of volatility you can stand and whether you are going to draw an income from the portfolio. Designing the right mix is a balancing act between two different types of risk. On one hand, you need to make sure that you outpace inflation and the destruction of the purchasing power of the dollar. Conversely, you must make sure that you don't take on a level of volatility that can cause problems during down markets. The next portion of this chapter examines the five types of time horizons that drive portfolio construction, and the purpose of each in helping investors achieve their needs and goals.

## The Five Time Horizons

**One Year or Less.** If you will need money in less than one year, it is a good idea to take little or no market risk. Historically, the stock market goes down one out of every three years. This leads to a high probability that your initial investment could be worth less money just when you need it. In addition, stocks also tend to go down at the worst possible times—right when you have an emergency or a need for money. If you are laid off, it is usually because the economy takes a dip, which is preceded by a market decline. In other words, the market tends to go down BEFORE economic problems are evident. If you know you'll need money to buy a car, pay college tuition, make a down-payment on property, or have any other short term goal in the next year, you are best served by putting that money in an account that will be worth no less than what you put into it.

The vehicle you choose will depend on how sure you are of timing your money needs. For example, if you know that you'll need the money in nine months, you might take out a nine-month CD at the local bank. That way you will know exactly how much interest you'll receive and when you can get your money back without a penalty. Since many CDs have a penalty for early withdrawal, the banks often pay a higher interest to compensate investors for increased risk if rates rise, and for having their funds tied up. I have found that CDs can be flexible and that banks will negotiate interest rates and maturity dates

It's nice to know when you'll need money and be able to plan accordingly, but this is not a perfect world. So, what if you're not sure exactly when you'll need the money? In those cases, you may choose to put the short-term money in a money market account or a savings account. Often these accounts are highly liquid, allowing you access through check writing privileges. Online banks and mutual fund companies frequently offer competitive interest rates for these liquid accounts. Just a word of caution: Be careful when the interest rate appears to be too good to be true. Some financial institutions have been known to take imprudent risks with investors' money just so they can advertise a high interest rate. Greed can get us in all kinds of trouble if we're not careful. The safest types of money market funds are backed by government debt for the reason we discussed—they can print money.

**One to Three Years: Conservative.** If you need the investment back in one to three years, then it may be advisable to put a small amount in the stock market. Typically, for short time horizons like this, I advise putting up to twenty-five percent into stocks. While it is possible that such a mix can go down slightly over a one-year period, it is rare for such an allocation to be worth less two or three years out. As you will see, the portfolio mix may consist of a mixture of cash and bonds maturing in a year or less, and five-year (or intermediate), bonds as well as stocks of different sized companies.

**Three to Five Years: Moderate.** The next time horizon is three to five years. If you have a goal that requires money four years from today, you could slightly increase your holdings of stocks. This time horizon allows you to put up to fifty percent of your money in the stock market. While there is more volatility expected with this mix, the fact that there is more time before the money is needed makes the risk easier to bear. Longer time horizons increase the risks of inflation and its destruction of purchasing power, so adding more stocks can help offset that risk.

**Six to Nine Years: Growth.** If your goal for the return of your money is six to nine years, you can now increase your stock holdings up to seventy-five percent of the portfolio. The growth mix also works for people with longer time horizons who are more comfortable with lower stock market exposure. Because bonds often move in the opposite direction of stocks, the difference between the expected return of a growth mix and an all-stock portfolio is not as large as you might imagine. This divergent price movement not only controls volatility, but it also allows an opportunity to gain more of the benefits of rebalancing.

As a side note, remember that we use this strategy to bring the portfolio back to its original target mix. When we have more divergent price movement, the result is greater opportunity to buy low and sell high. What a concept!

**Ten Plus Years: Aggressive.** For the longest time horizons you can put most, if not all, of the portfolio in stocks. The primary goal of an aggressive mix is to have maximum capital appreciation potential. This type of mix tends to give you the lowest long-term exposure to inflation risk. As you will see, the potential— historically speaking—for negative returns can be significant for an investor in this type of asset mix. If you can ride out these rough patches, however, the rewards can be great.

## The Mixes

Now we'll take a look at a practical application of the different timelines. The following chart shows the percentages to be invested in each asset class with each of the four objectives (in excess of one year) that we've just outlined.[41]

| SAMPLE ASSET CLASS MIXES PERCENT OF PORTFOLIO | | | | |
|---|---|---|---|---|
| ASSET CLASSES | CONSERVATIVE | MODERATE | GROWTH | AGGRESSIVE |
| **FIXED INCOME** | | | | |
| Cash Equivalents | 2.00% | 2.00% | 2.00% | 2.00% |
| Short Term Fixed | 36.50% | 24.00% | 11.50% | 1.50% |
| Intermediate Term Bonds | 36.50% | 24.00% | 11.50% | 1.50% |
| Long Term Bonds | 0.00% | 0.00% | 0.00% | 0.00% |
| Sub Total Fixed Income | 75.00% | 50.00% | 25.00% | 5.00% |
| **U.S. EQUITY** | | | | |
| Large Stocks | 2.61% | 4.50% | 6.37% | 7.50% |
| Large Value Stocks | 5.25% | 9.00% | 12.75% | 15.00% |
| Small Stocks | 5.26% | 9.00% | 12.75% | 15.00% |
| Small Value Stocks | 4.38% | 7.50% | 10.63% | 12.50% |
| Sub Total U.S. Equity | 17.50% | 30.00% | 42.50% | 50.00% |
| **INTERNATIONAL EQUITY** | | | | |
| Large Stocks | 2.65% | 7.00% | 11.38% | 15.75% |
| Small Stocks | 4.85% | 13.00% | 21.12% | 29.25% |
| Sub Total Int'l Equity | 7.50% | 20.00% | 32.50% | 45.00% |
| GRAND TOTAL | 100% | 100% | 100% | 100% |

If you choose an *aggressive* portfolio mix, then 7.5% of your portfolio should be invested in large U.S. stocks, 15% should go into large value stocks and small stocks, etc. Note that if you are attempting to allocate a workplace retirement plan, your investment provider may require that your mix percentages be expressed in round numbers. If that is the case, just round off to the nearest percent.

## International's Role in Your Mix

One important part of your asset allocation decision is the international side. In determining the appropriate mix for you, you may encounter a problem in the area of asset class availability. I am regularly faced with having to compensate for missing asset categories in my clients' retirement plans. And more often than not, the international side of the portfolio is severely lacking. In that case, I must allocate a larger percentage to the the available international asset class (usually large international growth). I will often back off on the percentage of international exposure versus U.S. exposure due to the limited number of international choices available.

Those of you with more investing experience may have noticed that some areas of international markets are missing, including international small value, international large value, and emerging markets (large, small, and value). They are missing because the available data on those areas doesn't go back far enough. It's important to let people see how their respective portfolios would have performed during both good and bad financial times, but much of the data on these other asset classes starts after the big market downturn in 1973 and 1974.

As a rule, I typically limit emerging markets to 15% of the total allocation dedicated to international. And I also place limits on emerging markets within the international category. Emerging markets can be extremely volatile, so don't succumb to the temptation to put too much of your money there. They can be subject to high levels of market and political risk.

I typically place more emphasis on the value side of the international equation. This is because there tends to be more divergent price movement between U.S. stocks and their international counterparts on the value side. Again, you may not even have options available in these areas if you are allocating a 401(k) or other workplace plan. But if so, it is important to be aware of the risks and benefits of using international stocks in your mix. However, if that asset class is available, it is important to understand the benefits of using it in your portfolio mix.

## The Rebalancing Act

The process of rebalancing is fairly simple; I'll use an example to explain the necessary steps. Let's say that you have a portfolio with $100,000 in it. If your intent is to have 10% of your money in large U.S. growth stocks and another 10% in small U.S. growth stocks, then you would put $10,000 (10% of $100,000) in each area. Let's say that one year later your investments are worth $120,000 due to market movements and additional deposits.

Simply multiply your target percentages by the total account value and compare the result with the actual balances. For instance, if your target for holding large U.S. growth stocks and small U.S. growth stocks is 10%, then you should have $12,000 in each area (or 10% of the new balance of $120,000).

If small companies are taking up $14,000 of the portfolio and large companies are still only taking up $10,000 of it, then you need to sell $2,000 worth of small companies and buy more of the large company fund.

This will likely be the direct opposite of what all your friends will be doing. They will be watching the news reports about the recent top performing stocks and how great they are doing. That will tempt them to buy more of the fund that you are selling. That is precisely why it is so difficult to discipline yourself to rebalance a portfolio. It is human nature to worry about missing something. We hear about people getting rich and try to jump on board with the latest investment craze— but it's usually too late.

As you can imagine, the math is rarely as simple as the previous example, but don't worry about getting the exact numbers. This is one area of life (like horse shoes and hand grenades) where close counts. As long as you bring the portfolio back close to the original targets, then you will gain the benefits that rebalancing offers.

Since taxes are not an issue in retirement plan rebalancing, you won't have to worry about how long you've held each asset category. (Remember, the tax rate on assets sold before they are held for one year can be higher than they are for assets held for over a year.) Typically, I recommend looking at your portfolio at least once a year for rebalancing. I find that most people don't like to spend a lot of time on their investments, so more frequent adjustments are usually not welcome. I have yet to meet an investor who relishes the thought of rebalancing based on deviations from the targets that I described in the previous chapter.

## Another Look at Time Horizons

Earlier I described each portfolio in terms of a specified time horizon before you may need your money back. For instance, the *aggressive* mix was designed for people who have at least ten years before they need all of their money back. Another way to look at time horizons is to determine how long you can go without a return. Let's say a client has a goal to buy a lake house in ten years, and they have $20,000 set aside for that goal. The question I like to ask them is: "Would you be happy if you had no more money than you started with ten years from now?" The answer from most people is a definitive "NO." Then I'll ask, "Would it be a complete disaster?" The answer again (but not as enthusiastically) is "no."

That is an important point. The investment industry tries to paint a Pollyannic view of the risks of investing. They try to appeal to greed and get you to think about how rich you'll become if you buy their products. But as we've seen, the truth is that markets go through long, painful declines. If we don't mentally prepare ourselves for that possibility, we will be tempted to bail out of our portfolio at the worst possible time. It is another example of why people sell low and sabotage their investment plans. Let me illustrate:

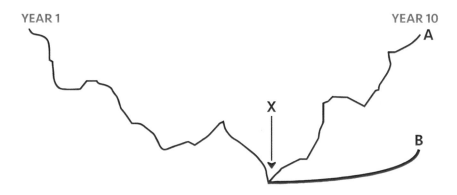

Let's say that you invest in year one in an *aggressive*, all-stock portfolio (portfolio A) and a severe, worldwide shock occurred. If you had no concept of time horizons, you might be driven to sell at point X and throw your money into a "safe" portfolio of CDs, illustrated as the bold line B. The result is that you've lost a good portion of your original investment. While there are no guarantees that the stock portfolio would have recovered, there are only three ten-year periods in the last ninety-two years during which the S&P 500 lost value. Two were during the Great Depression and one was from 2000-2009, and in all cases the losses were less than one percent per year. There were some pretty decent jumps in the market during the heart of the Depression as well, so even bad times can be accompanied by good stock returns. It's also worth noting that in the 2000-2009 period, greater diversification would have actually created a respectable gain.

Losses don't last forever because companies and their directors find some way to get back to profitability. After the Depression, that turnaround happened during World War II. Cars and washing machines weren't selling well, so companies changed production to tanks and airplanes to support the war effort.

That is why stocks climbed so rapidly during the early forties. While an investor who held on would have recovered all of their losses from the Depression downturn, an investor who bailed out and moved to an investment earning 3% per year would have had to wait over 400 years to recover all of their lost value. The turnarounds do come—and it's our job to hang on until they do.

## Asset Mixes and Incomes

People often ask me how it's possible to take an income from a stock portfolio that suddenly declines. The fear of a big market decline is all too real to investors who must live off of their life savings. To explain this I often ask, "What is the market anyway?" Most answer that it is large U.S. stocks or more often, the Dow. Investors must remember that the Dow is comprised of just thirty stocks, while a well-diversified portfolio should have well over 10,000 stocks.

A well-diversified portfolio should also contain a large portion of its money in bonds. Bonds don't move in lock step with stocks. Investors often run from stocks to bonds after a stock market decline. It's a move called the flight to quality, and it causes them to lock in their losses. They see bonds as a safe haven during market uncertainty, and their move to bonds often boosts their price. If and when the general direction of stocks is down, the stock portion of the portfolio may go down more than the bonds go up, causing the total portfolio value to go down temporarily. This is when we take income from the bond segment of the portfolio. (It is important to note that when stocks go down in value, longer term bonds may also go down. Their movement, however, is not by the same amounts and not at the same time.)

Studies show that an investor can take 4% to 5% of a portfolio's value out each year and be assured their money will not run out. Many of the studies recommend holding no less than 50% of the money in stocks. Will there be times when you take money out in a declining market? Yes, but that's why we hold bonds. Can things go wrong in the stock markets that have never happened before? Absolutely, but fixed income investments (CDs, etc.) can collapse too—and they have. Germany, Argentina, and Chile are just a few examples of economies that have gone through great difficulty in all areas of the market.

Even without a collapse in a country's currency, history doesn't provide a promising prospect for good results when investing long-term money in short- term investments like CDs and money markets. The long-term returns of these vehicles—even in this country—are barely above the inflation rate. They are negative after taxes are taken into account. On the other hand, stock market returns have exceeded 7% above inflation over the long run. It is not unusual to see 30% to 50% returns during a stock market recovery after a big decline. This increase more than makes up for the negative returns experienced during bear markets.

Keep in mind there is no such thing as life without risk. As much as humans dislike the unknown, risk only really ends when we die.

## Taking an Income

One of the most logical ways to take an income from your investments is to use the "multiple wells" approach. My father thought of this analogy when I was explaining the approach to him one day:

Let's say that I have spread my money among ten different areas of the market, like having ten wells, each with a different level of fresh water. I don't expect each area to perform well every year. For example, in 1998, U.S. large growth companies had the best returns, so the large growth well would be the highest. In 1999, the winner was emerging markets. In 2000, large U.S. value stocks did well. In 2001, small U.S. stocks had a good year. In 2002, after the 9/11 tragedy, government bonds were one of the only safe havens. Since the goal of investing is to buy low and sell high, I want to take my income from the area that is over-represented in my portfolio. It's like drawing from the well with the highest water level. If small stocks just had a stellar year, then I should take a part of my income by selling some of them. Technically, taking the money from cash and then rebalancing the portfolio accomplishes the same thing—and the effect will be virtually identical. In essence, the wells approach takes the emotion out of investing and allows stocks time to recover when markets are down.

We've just discussed how investors' time horizons play a critical role in choosing the most effective types of investments for their goals. The next chapter takes on another factor that is a harder to measure and varies more widely than the different time horizons—and that is expectations. We will discuss investors' individual expectations and how they play a vital role in our investment futures.

## Summary

- For most investors, choosing a portfolio mix consists of picking mutual funds with the best track record, called the grocery store approach to investing.

- The primary way to set a goal that leads to creating the proper investment mix involves choosing a time horizon.

- If you will need money in less than one year, it is a good idea to take little or no market risk. In this case, you should follow a year or less time horizon.

- If you need the investment back in one to three years, then it may be advisable to put a small amount in the stock market, up to twenty-five percent.

- If you have a goal that requires money four years from today, you could slightly increase your holdings of stocks, up to fifty percent.

- If your goal for the return of your money is six to nine years, you can now increase your stock holdings up to seventy-five percent of the portfolio.

- For the longest time horizon (ten plus years) you can put most, if not all, of the portfolio in stocks. The primary goal with this type of mix is to have maximum capital appreciation potential.

- In determining your appropriate mix, you may encounter a problem in the area of asset class availability, particularly on the international side.

- Most investors are tempted by the recent top performing asset category, which is why it is so difficult to discipline yourself to rebalance a portfolio as cautiously and as logically as possible, and typically not more often than once a year.

- Another way to look at time horizons is to determine how long you can go without a return.

- Diversified portfolios should also contain a large portion of the money in bonds, as this helps offset stock movement because bonds don't move in lock step with stocks.

- One of the best ways to take an income from your investments is to use the multiple-wells approach. The wells approach takes the emotion out of investing and allows stocks time to recover when markets are down.

## Quick Quiz

1. Choosing a portfolio mix often consists of picking mutual funds with the best track record. What is this method called and why is it called that?

2. What is the first thing to determine before selecting your investments?

3. What are some other considerations in the investment selection process?

4. What are the five different time horizons?

5. Historically, the stock market goes down one out of every _____ years.

6. Be careful when the interest rate appears to be too good to be true. Why must you exercise caution in these cases?

7. If you are investing for one to three years, what percentage of that investment might go into stocks?

8. If you have a goal that requires money four years from today, what should you do in relation to the percentage of stocks in your portfolio?

9. What is the primary goal with an aggressive mix?

10. What particular part of your asset allocation is most often overlooked?

11. Typically, I recommend looking at your portfolio at least _____ for _____ rebalancing.

12. One method to determine what mix you should choose is to pick the right time horizon for you. What is another way to determine what type of allocation to choose?

13. Diversified portfolios designed to provide income for an investor should also contain a large portion of the money in bonds. Why?

14. One of the most logical ways to take an income from your investments is to use the multiple wells approach. What does that mean?

## CHAPTER FOURTEEN

# THE ROLE OF EXPECTATIONS
# IN INVESTING

# The Role of Expectations in Investing

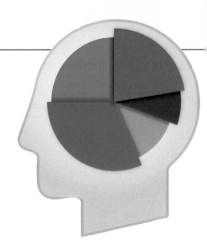

**The most common reason that people change** their portfolio is a lack of appropriate expectations. Although the phrase may apply to some areas of life, ignorance is *not* bliss when it comes to investing. That is why successful investors must understand how their portfolios will react to different types of markets. I like to use the following chart to explain this idea to clients:

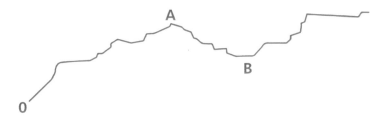

It isn't through the A type market conditions that we question our investment strategies. Nobody worries when the market is going straight up. In fact, we tend to feel bulletproof and get excited about throwing more money into our mutual funds during those periods. It is during the B times that we become restless and make changes. We must have a strong educational foundation BEFORE we invest at point 0.

I use the following formula to further explain this concept: $(I + E) \times M > C$. That is, our Instincts plus our Emotions outweigh (are greater than) the Cognitive part of our minds. This concept gets magnified or multiplied by the media (M). The members of the investment industry tend to starve the cognitive parts of our minds and prey upon our emotions and instincts. And since they make the majority of their money on transactions and trades, they have a vested interest in our continuous buying and selling of stocks and bonds, even when our brains scream, "Leave your investments alone!"

## Historical Returns

The model portfolios we covered in the last chapter are designed to maximize expected returns for a given level of risk. When coaching clients, I show them the year-to-year returns of such portfolios from 1973 until the present. Here is what that chart looks like:[42]

| HISTORICAL PORTFOLIO RETURNS | | | | |
|---|---|---|---|---|
| Year | Conservative | Moderate | Growth | Aggressive |
| 1973 | -0.52% | -6.42% | -12.32% | -16.84% |
| 1974 | -0.66% | -8.69% | -16.73% | -23.23% |
| 1975 | 19.09% | 30.01% | 40.92% | 49.36% |
| 1976 | 16.11% | 20.75% | 25.41% | 28.15% |
| 1977 | 8.49% | 15.98% | 23.44% | 30.51% |
| 1978 | 10.22% | 17.55% | 24.86% | 31.74% |
| 1979 | 11.02% | 13.66% | 16.31% | 17.64% |
| 1980 | 12.13% | 17.54% | 22.94% | 27.42% |
| 1981 | 10.73% | 8.91% | 7.09% | 5.38% |
| 1982 | 22.38% | 20.30% | 18.23% | 15.81% |
| 1983 | 14.36% | 20.48% | 26.61% | 31.48% |
| 1984 | 11.59% | 10.13% | 8.67% | 7.64% |
| 1985 | 21.66% | 29.72% | 37.76% | 45.01% |
| 1986 | 15.88% | 22.68% | 29.47% | 36.13% |
| 1987 | 5.03% | 7.73% | 10.41% | 13.57% |
| 1988 | 10.97% | 15.92% | 20.88% | 24.89% |
| 1989 | 14.18% | 16.95% | 19.71% | 21.98% |
| 1990 | 2.41% | -4.62% | -11.64% | -17.32% |
| 1991 | 16.10% | 18.69% | 21.29% | 22.61% |
| 1992 | 7.44% | 6.90% | 6.38% | 4.93% |
| 1993 | 11.51% | 16.22% | 20.92% | 24.95% |
| 1994 | -0.48% | 0.94% | 2.37% | 3.85% |
| 1995 | 15.97% | 18.15% | 20.34% | 21.32% |
| 1996 | 7.06% | 9.52% | 11.98% | 13.56% |
| 1997 | 10.67% | 12.21% | 13.76% | 14.00% |
| 1998 | 8.56% | 9.39% | 10.22% | 11.02% |
| 1999 | 5.69% | 10.78% | 15.86% | 20.22% |
| 2000 | 7.64% | 4.55% | 1.46% | -1.44% |
| 2001 | 6.49% | 4.21% | 1.93% | -0.60% |
| 2002 | 2.01% | -3.33% | -8.67% | -12.62% |
| 2003 | 14.13% | 26.53% | 38.92% | 48.91% |

| 2004 | 6.53% | 12.10% | 17.66% | 22.40% |
|---|---|---|---|---|
| 2005 | 4.38% | 7.53% | 10.67% | 13.51% |
| 2006 | 8.32% | 13.10% | 17.88% | 21.80% |
| 2007 | 5.91% | 4.48% | 3.04% | 2.18% |
| 2008 | -3.43% | -16.02% | -28.62% | -38.88% |
| 2009 | 8.53% | 18.29% | 28.05% | 36.07% |
| 2010 | 7.74% | 11.43% | 15.12% | 18.00% |
| 2011 | 1.10% | -2.76% | -6.60% | -9.86% |
| 2012 | 5.85% | 10.61% | 15.37% | 19.09% |
| 2013 | 7.90% | 16.67% | 25.45% | 32.07% |
| 2014 | 2.10% | 2.00% | 1.90% | 1.50% |
| 2015 | -0.31% | -1.00% | -1.70% | -1.98% |
| 2016 | 5.95% | 9.49% | 13.04% | 15.33% |
| 2017 | 5.53% | 10.76% | 15.99% | 20.55% |
| Annualized Return | 8.38% | 10.24% | 11.83% | 12.87% |
| Standard Deviation | 4.70% | 7.94% | 11.60% | 14.63% |

As you can see, the range of returns varies significantly based on the amount of exposure to stocks in the portfolio. As we go left to right—or conservative to aggressive— the standard deviation (or risk) of the portfolio rises as well as the expected return. Each portfolio's standard deviation is shown on the bottom row of the chart.

We start with 1973 and 1974 because stocks dropped significantly in those two years. This period represents the worst market conditions since the Great Depression. As some of you may recall, the 70's were the days of the OPEC Oil Embargo and rapidly rising gas prices. Later, we see a similar period in 2008 and early 2009 with the banking crisis. These events had a dramatic effect on corporate profits and drove stock prices down significantly. It is helpful to look at this chart and imagine how you might react if your portfolio experienced such volatility. Of course, sometimes it is difficult to be honest with ourselves about the risk that we can handle. It's like saying that we know how we'll react in an auto accident because we've been through one in an arcade game, but when market meltdowns actually occur, the TV shows, magazines and newspapers all tell us the sky is falling and the end is near, making it quite difficult to stay disciplined.

The chart on the next page depicts how a dollar would have grown if it were invested using the mixes in the model portfolios:[43]

| GROWTH OF $1 IN PORTFOLIO MIXES 1973-2017 | | | |
|---|---|---|---|
| YEAR | CONSERVATIVE | MODERATE | GROWTH | AGGRESSIVE |
| 01/01/1973 | $1.00 | $1.00 | $1.00 | $1.00 |
| 12/31/1973 | $0.99 | $0.94 | $0.88 | $0.83 |
| 12/31/1974 | $0.99 | $0.85 | $0.73 | $0.64 |
| 12/31/1975 | $1.18 | $1.11 | $1.03 | $0.95 |
| 12/31/1976 | $1.37 | $1.34 | $1.29 | $1.22 |
| 12/31/1977 | $1.48 | $1.56 | $1.59 | $1.59 |
| 12/31/1978 | $1.63 | $1.83 | $1.99 | $2.10 |
| 12/31/1979 | $1.81 | $2.08 | $2.31 | $2.47 |
| 12/31/1980 | $2.03 | $2.44 | $2.84 | $3.15 |
| 12/31/1981 | $2.25 | $2.66 | $3.05 | $3.32 |
| 12/31/1982 | $2.76 | $3.20 | $3.60 | $3.84 |
| 12/31/1983 | $3.15 | $3.86 | $4.56 | $5.05 |
| 12/31/1984 | $3.52 | $4.25 | $4.95 | $5.44 |
| 12/31/1985 | $4.28 | $5.51 | $6.82 | $7.89 |
| 12/31/1986 | $4.96 | $6.76 | $8.84 | $10.74 |
| 12/31/1987 | $5.21 | $7.28 | $9.76 | $12.20 |
| 12/31/1988 | $5.78 | $8.44 | $11.79 | $15.23 |
| 12/31/1989 | $6.60 | $9.87 | $14.12 | $18.58 |
| 12/31/1990 | $6.76 | $9.42 | $12.47 | $15.36 |
| 12/31/1991 | $7.85 | $11.17 | $15.13 | $18.83 |
| 12/31/1992 | $8.43 | $11.95 | $16.10 | $19.76 |
| 12/31/1993 | $9.40 | $13.88 | $19.46 | $24.69 |
| 12/31/1994 | $9.36 | $14.01 | $19.92 | $25.64 |
| 12/31/1995 | $10.85 | $16.56 | $23.97 | $31.11 |
| 12/31/1996 | $11.62 | $18.13 | $26.85 | $35.33 |
| 12/31/1997 | $12.85 | $20.35 | $30.54 | $40.27 |
| 12/31/1998 | $13.95 | $22.26 | $33.66 | $44.71 |
| 12/31/1999 | $14.75 | $24.66 | $39.00 | $53.75 |
| 12/31/2000 | $15.88 | $25.78 | $39.57 | $52.98 |
| 12/31/2001 | $16.91 | $26.86 | $40.33 | $52.66 |
| 12/31/2002 | $17.25 | $25.97 | $36.83 | $46.02 |
| 12/31/2003 | $19.69 | $32.86 | $51.17 | $68.53 |
| 12/31/2004 | $20.97 | $36.83 | $60.20 | $83.87 |
| 12/31/2005 | $21.89 | $39.60 | $66.63 | $95.21 |
| 12/31/2006 | $23.71 | $44.79 | $78.54 | $115.96 |
| 12/31/2007 | $25.11 | $46.80 | $80.92 | $118.49 |
| 12/31/2008 | $24.25 | $39.30 | $57.77 | $72.42 |

| 12/31/2009 | $26.32 | $46.49 | $73.97 | $98.54 |
|---|---|---|---|---|
| 12/31/2010 | $28.36 | $51.80 | $85.16 | $116.28 |
| 12/31/2011 | $28.67 | $50.37 | $79.53 | $104.82 |
| 12/31/2012 | $30.34 | $55.72 | $91.75 | $124.83 |
| 12/31/2013 | $32.74 | $65.01 | $115.10 | $164.86 |
| 12/31/2014 | $33.43 | $66.31 | $117.29 | $167.34 |
| 12/31/2015 | $33.33 | $65.64 | $115.30 | $164.04 |
| 12/31/2016 | $35.31 | $71.88 | $130.33 | $189.18 |
| 12/31/2017 | $37.33 | $79.70 | $151.24 | $228.08 |
| $100,000 invested would have grown to: | $3,732,902.58 | $7,970,198.16 | $15,123,753.86 | $22,807,729.98 |

The bottom line shows the growth of a hypothetical deposit of $100,000 at the beginning of the period. People are amazed at the level of returns the market can deliver without the aid of any brilliant stock picking or market timing.

## Judging Your Portfolio

Now that we know the criteria for picking the best investment strategy for your portfolio, we'll discuss how it is doing. There are two ways to judge your portfolio's performance; The first method is called the **Macro Method** of sizing up performance. With the Macro Method, you must look at whether your portfolio performed within expectations as a whole. In other words, look at the return over a calendar year and compare it to the range of returns you expected from the portfolio. You may recall that you can get an idea of what to expect by looking at the standard deviation (the yo-yo string analogy found in Chapter Ten) of the portfolio, and based on that, you can calculate the range of returns that the portfolio might deliver. This important tool allows you to relax during stressful economic times.

For example, if you used an aggressive mix, your expected return is approximately 8% above inflation after expenses. (If inflation is 4%, then you have a long-term expected return of 12%. If it's 2%, then the expected long-term return is 10%.) Simply calculate the overall range of returns using the gross return (10% or 12% in this example) as the base. Using 12%, if your standard deviation were eighteen, then you would expect—with a 95% level of confidence—that the portfolio won't return more than 48% [12 + (18 x 2)]. On the down side, you could see a negative 24% in one year [12 – (18 x 2)]. As long as your portfolio is in between those two numbers (negative 24% and positive 48%), then you know the portfolio is performing within the range of expectations. A 95% level of confidence means that only 5% of historical returns would have been outside these ranges.

The second way to judge performance, called the Micro Method, is to look at each mutual fund and make sure that it matches the return (within reason) of the asset class it attempts to replicate. It's called the Micro Method because it allows you to focus on the smaller picture or "parts" of your portfolio. For instance, you may want to compare the return of your large company U.S. fund to the performance of the S&P 500. If the fund had significant under-performance, there is a problem. Despite what you may think, though, you don't want the fund to outperform significantly either. If the S&P 500 goes down 10% and the fund goes up 10%, then you know that the manager gambled with your money and got lucky. If they can gamble and get lucky, then they can surely gamble and get unlucky.

Some asset classes are easier to replicate with mutual funds (like large U.S. and large international), so this process of benchmarking is not a perfect science. I typically just look at each fund and compare it to its index counter-part. As long as you exercise care in choosing your funds when assembling the portfolio, you won't likely see a great deal of difference between the returns of your funds and their respective indexes (or the asset classes they are tracking).

Here is a list of some of the indexes that I use as a basis of comparison and the asset classes they represent:

- S&P 500 – Large U.S. stocks

- Barra U.S. Large Value (or Russell 1000 Value) – Large U.S. Value stocks

- Russell 2000 – Small U.S. stocks

- Russell 2000 Value – Small U.S. Value stocks

- EAFE Index – International Large stocks

Using the Macro and Micro Methods of judging your portfolio provides a powerful tool for the investor to create peace of mind. Far too often, we are tempted to make changes in our mutual funds when no change is war-ranted. Using these evaluative methods gives us a "permission slip" to just leave things alone and let market forces do their thing. It gives us confidence that everything is going just as it should and that we don't have to lose sleep over worrying that we made bad choices.

In the end, that confidence will be an important ingredient in your success. Confident investors are disciplined investors, and disciplined investors are far more likely to be successful investors.

## Summary

- The most common reason that people change their portfolios is a lack of appropriate expectations

- $(I + E)$ x $M > C$, which means our "Instincts" plus our "Emotions" magnified by the "Media" outweigh the "Cognitive" part of our minds, and the investment industry tends to prey upon this fact.

- There are two ways to judge your portfolio's performance: 1) The Macro Method 2) The Micro Method. Both are powerful tools to help you create peace of mind.

- With the Macro Method of sizing up performance, you must look at whether your portfolio performed within expectations as a whole. In other words, look at the return over a calendar year and compare it to the range of returns you expected from the portfolio.

- The second way to judge performance, called the Micro Method, is to look at each mutual fund and make sure that it matches the return (within reason) of the asset class it attempts to replicate. This method is called Micro because it allows you to focus on the small parts of your portfolio.

- As long as you exercise care in choosing your funds when assembling the portfolio, you won't likely see a great deal of difference between the returns of your funds and their respective indexes. Here is a list of some of the indexes to use as a basis of comparison and the asset classes they represent: S&P 500— Large U.S. stocks; Barra U.S. large value (or Russell 1000 Value)—Large U.S. value stocks; Russell 2000—Small U.S. stocks; Russell 2000 Value—Small U.S. value stocks; EAFE Index—International large stocks

- Always remember that disciplined investors are far more likely to be successful investors.

## Quick Quiz

1. What is the most common reason why people change their portfolios?

2. Although the phrase may apply to some areas of life, ignorance is _____ when it comes to investing.

3. In the following formula, what do the letters stand for: (I + E) x M > C?

4. Who stands to gain the most from people making decisions based heavily on emotion and instinct?

5. What is the Macro Method?

6. How does the second method of portfolio performance, the Micro Method, differ from the Macro Method?

7. True or False: Using evaluative methods such as the Macro and Micro Methods gives us a permission slip to just leave things alone and let market forces do their thing.

8. Confident investors are disciplined investors, and disciplined investors are far more likely to be _____ investors.

## CHAPTER FIFTEEN

# FREQUENTLY ASKED QUESTIONS

# Frequently Asked Questions

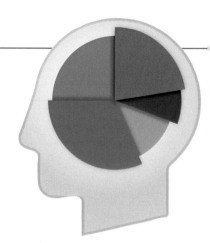

**The topic of investing is wide ranging** and involves many different and sometimes unrelated topics. Consequently, some of the questions I receive from my clients and on my radio show don't fit the neat confines of a book chapter. That is why I decided to include a separate chapter to answer common questions I hear regarding investing and financial planning. The following are a handful of those important FAQs that belong in this book:

## Q: Are P/E Ratios useful in determining if markets are overvalued?

Actually, I've performed studies that show the Cyclically Adjusted P/E ratios (Schiller CAPE) aren't helpful in predicting future market direction. Logic seems to tell us that an above-average P/E ratio means that stocks are over-priced, but the data doesn't support that. As you can see from the following chart, there is no predictable pattern when you look at Cyclically Adjusted P/E ratios and returns. Each dot represents a combination of the P/E data in one year and what the market returned the next year.

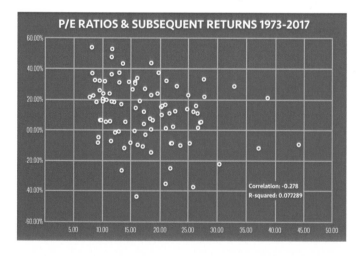

If current stock prices divided by the ten-year average of corporate earnings (CAPE) and future returns were related to each other, then there would be a straight line through this graph. That is, when prices are high compared to earnings, the next year's returns would be low or even negative. The fact that these dots are randomly scattered suggests that no such relationship exists. And this is exactly what we would expect, since the stock markets are so effective at properly pricing securities.

For those of you who are curious about why this happens, it has a lot to do with earnings growth and/or cost of capital requirements. When earnings grow rapidly, investors are simply willing to pay more for stocks. They know that more money will (likely) come rolling in a few years down the road. At other times, such as when perceived risk is low, investors must pay more for earnings

## Q: Should I worry if my withdrawals from my portfolio start to eat into my principal?

When investors need to start drawing an income from their investments, they worry about dipping into their principal. Although their concern is expected and even valid, they must realize that this may be inevitable in a portfolio designed to outpace inflation. The only types of investment vehicles that won't suffer temporary negative returns are short-term fixed income investments like CDs or money market accounts. As you know, however, these investments will also do well to break even after inflation.

Any portfolio that has the ability to protect you against inflation will, from time to time, decrease in value. This is why you should always maintain some exposure to bonds and other fixed income investments. They serve as the source for spendable income when stock markets are in a downturn. Remember that downturns have always been temporary. In this book, I cited studies on levels of income that you could have historically drawn from a well-diversified investment portfolio. These studies include some exceedingly difficult times in our nation's history such as the Great Depression, World War II, the Korean War, the Vietnam War, the OPEC Oil Embargo, '08-'09 banking crisis, etc.

You will always have to contend with risk. The best you can do is make sure to have broad diversification.

## Q: Can this approach to investing be implemented with index funds?

Although it is not optimal, this approach can, and often is, implemented using index funds. Index funds are often used because investors know that the fund won't drift into other asset categories based on the whim of the manager. In other words, a small company index fund won't suddenly drift into investing in a large number of large U.S. growth stocks. Another positive attribute of indexes is that they generally avoid stock picking and market timing. I must say "generally" because more and more, funds with "index" in their names are being actively managed, so be careful around this word.

Assuming that you have found *true* indexes, you should be aware of several drawbacks when using this approach:

1. You may not be able to find index funds that give you access to several areas of the market, or they may not capture the asset class as well as other alternatives. For instance, it is difficult—if not impossible—to find well- diversified index funds that invest in international small or international small value stocks. Some emerging market categories may be hard to find as well. When I am forced to use indexes for my clients (in 401(k) plans or 529 plans), I often overweight large international stocks and the U.S. side of the portfolio to make up for the lack of asset class access.

2. Index funds often don't represent the asset classes you seek as well as other alternatives. For example, you may be able to find a U.S. value stock fund, but the fund may not be as "value" as you would like. I often find that the companies held by an index fund may be larger than optimal, or they may have a higher price-to-book value than normal due to capitalization weighting. Again, this is an area that can get complicated rather quickly. It is helpful to use an experienced advisor when choosing the proper investments.

3. Since indexes are reconstituted (stocks are changed within the index) on a regular basis, you will often incur trading costs that could have been avoided with funds that don't have to adhere to the index.

## Q: What role does gold play in your investing scheme? And how, if a person invests in gold, do they utilize it?

I don't recommend using gold as an investment—or any other commodities, for that matter. By definition an investment should involve the "cost of capital" concept. In other words, someone should be using your money and paying you for it. If you lend money to a bank, they pay you interest for it. If you buy stock, you get the rights to the company's future profits. If you buy gold, you own nothing but a commodity whose price rises and falls based on supply and demand. An ounce of gold would have bought a nice man's suit a hundred years ago, and it has about the same purchasing power today.

Many people claim that gold is a good alternative currency and owning it protects you in a severe crisis. Recently I read an article in which the author disputed this notion with some valid points. The author noted that if such a calamity were to occur, anarchy would break out. If someone found out that you had gold hidden in your back yard, it is quite possible that they would find a way to get it—and most likely through violent means. And all of this is first assuming that gold would even have value in the event of such a collapse in the financial system. Furthermore, consider why someone selling you gold based on its ability to protect you from currency collapse would be willing to take your dollars (currency) for their gold.

Finally, the author cautioned that it is often far easier to buy gold than to sell it. Unlike stocks and bonds, gold is awkward to trade. There are not only high costs to buy and sell gold, but you also have to consider the costs to ship and store it as well. It is usually only the dealers in gold who make the most money. This is how they afford all of the commercials on the radio and television, and those crafty infomercials are designed to appeal to your greed and your deepest fears.

## Q: When the economy is shaky, is it time to get out of the market?

Because we are driven to self-preservation, we try to predict predict the future direction of the market. Ironically, we have a tendency to attract into our lives the very things we fear most. When I played football in high school, I was so concerned about getting hurt that I "played it safe." The result was that I wasn't all that good and I got injured anyway. Jonathan, a Certified

Financial Planner® who works with me, said it's like learning to ride a motor-cycle. One of the first things you learn is to make sure you always look where you are going and where you want to go. Don't look at the ground or you will end up there.

In an effort to protect themselves from losing money in their investments, people try to guess where the market is going next. Here are a couple of diagrams I use to explain how things go wrong:

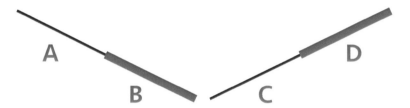

If the market goes down (the thin line A), we make up our minds that the future direction will be that as well (the thick line B). We actually do the same thing during up markets. When the market goes up (thin line C), we tend to believe that things will continue that way (thick line D).

So why does this happen? First, the media sees the same market movements and seeks to explain them. News hosts interview market participants who explain why the up or down movements occur. Investors then make buying or selling decisions, not realizing that all of the news has already been digested by the market and by now is reflected in stock prices. If the news is good, they will buy (at the new high prices). If it's bad news, they will sell (at the new low prices).

Market performance during different economic conditions is actually quite surprising. The following graph shows us that markets can actually move in the exact opposite direction of the Gross Domestic Product, a measure of the country's economic health.

The bottom line here is don't trust your gut or put the fate of your investments in the hands of the media and their scare tactics. Trust the numbers and go on facts. The economy will have bad times—and then it will improve. It is cyclical like everything else in life. If you pull out every time things look shaky, you will do nothing but harm your investments, and consequently, your retirement.

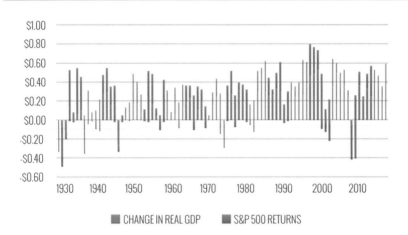

**CHANGE IN REAL GDP VS. S&P 500 RETURNS**

■ CHANGE IN REAL GDP    ■ S&P 500 RETURNS

## Q: If the market takes a big drop, is it a good time to buy stocks?

Historically speaking, most often the answer is yes. There is a concept in academic circles called the reversion to the mean. After a long negative return in the stock market, stocks will go through extraordinarily high returns. This is because the initial negative returns drag down the average return of the market, and very high returns are necessary to bring the market back in line with its long-term averages (or mean). It is debatable, though, whether the market will recover, and even if it did, it is impossible to figure out when the large returns will happen.

The reason is simple: History has a way of doing things differently the next time around. It's also impossible to know when the market has finished dropping. Investors are usually afraid and uncertain during downturns, and frequently they pay less for each dollar of profits they are likely to get. As a result they begin to expect even higher returns for themselves. It is a compensation for taking the risk of buying stocks when other investors won't.

It is interesting to note that this concept is nothing new. The Venetian Prestiti was a bond used to finance the republic's wars over 500 years ago and was traded much as stocks are traded today. According to historical data this investment had its highest returns in unstable times and its lowest returns when relative stability abounded.[44]

Since we don't really know for certain whether markets will skyrocket after a big fall, we must apply a point I made earlier in the book: Stocks always have a higher expected return than fixed income investments. Therefore, at any time, you should see higher returns from stocks. Just make sure your mix of stocks to bonds fits your time horizon.

## Q: I have an annuity that is supposed to protect my principal. Is this a good idea?

One of the basic tenets of investing is that risk and return are related. If you take more risk, you are usually rewarded with greater returns. Despite this basic principle of investing, many insurance agents and financial advisors sell products that are supposed to provide the investor with stock market returns without the downside risk potential. To make matters worse, some advisors use misleading tactics to sell insurance products to the unwary public.

Always remember that investing is about cost of capital. Investors allow others to use their money and want to get paid when they do so. The more risk involved with the use of their money, the greater the potential reward, but if there is no risk, investors cannot demand more return. Insurance companies aren't going to pay more than they have to for the privilege of using your money. Keep that in mind the next time an agent tries to sell you a certain product that has no risk.

It has always intrigued me that advisors don't see a fundamental flaw in the concept of a product that promises participation in market returns with no downside risk. The concept of car insurance is that a large group of people pay a small premium just in case tone of them has an accident and incurs a large loss. The problem with insuring investments is that a calamity in the investment markets would affect all participants. An insurance company would, more than likely, not survive the experience.

Companies who sell annuities restrict returns on these products in several different ways. One is through charging extremely high additional fees on top of the management fee. That is often the method used in variable annuity products. The fee is referred to as mortality and expense charges or M&E, and the expense can really dampen the upside of investment potential.

Equity-indexed annuities are more complicated. The insurance company may have a participation rate that lowers the return potential, and, often, the product's performance is tied to an index such as the S&P 500. If the participation rate is 7% and the index climbs 10%, then the investor gets just 7% of that growth.

Finally, the investor misses out on the portion of the market's return that comes from dividends paid by the underlying companies. The significance of this difference should not go unnoticed. According to data from Ibbotson and Associates and Standard and Poor's, Inc., $1 invested in the S&P 500 in 1960 would have grown to almost $260 by the end of 2017. However, if you remove dividends from the equation, that same dollar would have only grown to just over $46. As with many investment products on the market today, annuities are often far more financially rewarding for the salesperson than the end investor.

## Q: I am currently holding a large amount of stock, which I have held on to for a loss. Should I sell the stock (locking in the loss) and pick up an emerging market fund to help me regain my losses?

Yes, it is wise to get rid of the stock. As I often say, the thing that got you in trouble isn't likely to get you *out* of trouble. The expected return of a single stock is no higher than the expected return of all companies of like size and risk. Therefore, holding on to that stock in hopes that it will miraculously rebound is imprudent. It is much like a gambler who, after losing a significant amount of money, decides to continue gambling just until he breaks even.

Likewise, it is also not wise to put too much into emerging markets. Even though it is an asset category with a higher expected return over the long run, it could take a long time for that return to come to fruition. There are high political risks in emerging market countries, and property rights protections may be questionable. Just because an asset category has an above average expected return doesn't mean that the return will necessarily materialize. For instance, large U.S. stocks significantly outperformed small U.S. stocks through the entire decade of the 1980s, even though the small stock category has a higher expected return.

## Q: I work with a big, well-known company *that's* been around a long time. Shouldn't I feel confident that my investments are in good hands?

Maybe, maybe not. Take the firm's name with which you have your investments and enter it into an Internet search engine along with the words *lawsuit, settlement, misconduct,* or other such words. You'll probably find that every major firm has had some substantial missteps throughout its history. Unfortunately, the industry bar for prudent investing is set extremely low, and most companies can't (or won't) adequately supervise all of their advisors' activities. I have also found that in some cases, the advisor doesn't even recognize problems until it is too late. That is because the level of education required to enter the industry is minimal. In my experience, many of the largest and best-known firms have been party to some of the worst looking portfolios to ever cross my desk.

## Q: But this time it's different.

Each time we experience extreme market conditions, here comes the cry from investors, "But this has never happened before." We are afraid when we face unfamiliar circumstances, but we should remember: The specifics of a crisis are *always* new. It's always going to be different this time around.

Although I don't know what the market is doing as you read this sentence, I am sure something is happening somewhere that we've never experienced before. If the news is good, chances are the market responds positively and goes up as a result. However, if the news is bad, then stocks will likely go down, and that is the point I wish to address.

People panicked over the market crash of the early thirties. They probably said, "This has never happened before! People are losing their homes, unemployment is skyrocketing, crops are failing, international trade is decreasing, and the government is raising taxes." Then after the market went up significantly in the late thirties, people probably said, "There is a mad dictator on the loose in Europe with a huge army and he's invading several countries." In 1941 they said, "This has never happened before! Japan just attacked us on our own soil. They destroyed a huge part of our Navy, and it will take years to rebuild." Then came the early sixties. "Oh my, the Soviet Union put nuclear missiles in Cuba right off our shores. This could be a disaster."

And it seems that unprecedented events never stopped. After the sixties, we faced a new set of challenges with The Vietnam War and the war protestors (with their rampant pharmaceutical usage). After the war we experienced the Oil Crisis years and the threat of completely running out of our main energy source. Don't forget about Stagflation of the latter seventies, the Gulf War, the Asian Economic Crisis, 911, the Iraq War, and the banking crisis.

Roseanne Roseannadanna from *Saturday Night Live* was right when she quipped, "It's always something."

There is always something completely new going on. We usually don't make the same exact mistake multiple times; as humans, we like to foul things up a little differently each time. The one thing that all of these events have in common is that we recovered from them. The best thing to do is expect the unexpected and don't let events change your strategy.

## Q: Given all the discussions of energy independence and imminent use of alternative forms of energy, is this is a good time to invest in alternative energy stocks?

Don't ever concentrate on a specific industry with the idea that you know something that everyone else doesn't know. An excellent example of how this can work against you is cell phones. It is no secret that the cell phone industry has been a huge success over the past several years. With that in mind, one would think that the company who pioneered that technology—Motorola—would have benefited greatly from that growth. However, over the past fifteen years ending in December 2017, Motorola's stock underperformed the S&P 500 by over 3% per year.

## Q: I have heard some investment experts say to follow a top-down approach to stock picking. What does that mean?

Top-down investing involves stock picking and market timing to determine how specific companies or industries within the overall economy will benefit from current conditions. The investor assumes that they have information unknown to the rest of the market. As we've seen, this is not realistic.

## Q: What is a reverse stock split? Is it good for the shareholders?

To understand a reverse stock split, we must first understand a stock split. Let's say that we have a company with one million outstanding shares that are selling for $100 per share. The total value of our company is $100 million. If the company does a two-for-one stock split, the new share price would be $50 per share and the number of shares outstanding would be two million.

Nothing changes regarding the value of the company. It's a lot like cutting a pie in half. There is no change in the amount of pie, but the pieces are smaller.

Although many people believe that stock splits are good for returns, there is no evidence that this is the case. It simply makes the stock more affordable for smaller investors. Reverse stock splits work in the opposite fashion. If we had a company with a million outstanding shares selling at $10 per share, after a one-for- two (reverse) stock split, we would have 500,000 shares selling for $20 per share.

## Q: They say that institutional trading is what truly moves stock prices. Where can I see what these big players are doing?

It is true that much of the trading is done by big institutional investors. However, it won't do you much good to look at their activities. As we've seen, the big professional manager's success with stock picking is tenuous at best. Sometimes they might attempt to buy a stock before a big mutual fund buys it in order to benefit from the stock's price jump due to the temporary increase in demand. This technique is illegal however, and has gotten traders who have tried it in a lot of trouble.

## Q: What is "short interest" for a stock?

Short interest is the number of shares of a stock that have been sold short but haven't been repurchased. (Shorting stock is when a stock is borrowed, then sold in anticipation that it could be bought back in the future at a cheaper price and replaced.) Increased short interest is an indication that more investors believe the stock is headed down in value. I wouldn't advise using short interest to direct any investing decisions. It is just another form of market timing.

## Q: I've heard of researchers saying that Modern Portfolio Theory is outdated and no longer works. What do you say about that?

As you will recall, Modern Portfolio Theory states that a portfolio built with dissimilar asset classes tend to deliver higher expected returns for a given level of risk. This does not mean that asset classes will always move in dissimilar fashion. Periods of time when different areas of the market move together are often followed by articles stating that diversification, and, hence, Modern

Portfolio Theory is dead. Those nay-sayers tend to fade into obscurity when the market once again proves them wrong.

## Q: I am a brand new investor, and, quite frankly, I don't know what I'm doing. Common financial buzzwords are foreign to me, and the news scares me into not wanting to invest. What is the best way for me to get started?

Of course, the best first step to better investing is to become educated before putting your money into any investment vehicle. This book was written for that purpose. Next, I recommend working with a fee-only advisor; working with such an advisor ensures that the investment provider will not pay him or her. This is where you have to be careful. Since the financial industry is loosely regulated in the area of education requirements, you the investor must have a certain base level of knowledge about investing in order to discern the difference between a qualified and unqualified advisor.

So, filter all of the investment advice you hear through the academic evidence I have presented in this book. Ignore all predictions about the future. Become an active participant and understand as much as you can about your investment. Use discernment to be able to see truths from mere Wall Street myths. Then you will be a more confident investor and make informed, educated decisions based on information and logic rather than emotions and crafty marketing.

## Q: I've read a lot about working with a financial advisor who will act as a fiduciary (putting my interest before theirs) when giving me advice. What are your thoughts on this?

I've always recommended that investors work with advisors who adhere to a fiduciary standard in giving advice. However, I think it is only a good start and is not going to solve the issues that plague the financial industry.

When regulators like the Department of Labor began pushing for the fiduciary standard many years ago, I made the prediction (and I don't make many predictions) that it wouldn't work. I pointed out many times on my radio show that there were two likely outcomes in forcing advisors to be fiduciaries: One was that they would leave the business in droves because they didn't really *know* what was in the client's best interest. Most were trained to simply sell financial products to the public with little formal education. The second possible outcome, I predicted, was a watering down of the definition of fiduciary.

Back in 2016 I actually saw a study that showed that nearly 20% of financial advisors were considering leaving the industry due to impending fiduciary regulations. The first prediction was beginning to come true.[45]

What was more interesting to me was the study from the University of Indiana and University of Southern California "The Misguided Beliefs of Financial Advisors". The study found that "advisors trade frequently, chase returns, prefer expensive, actively managed funds, and underdiversify." Based on what you've read in this book, that's probably not much of a surprise. Here is the kicker: They not only do that with their client's money, *but with their own as well.* I found another line in the abstract of the study to be rather eye-opening as well: "Advisors do not strategically hold expensive portfolios only to convince clients to do the same; they continue to do so after they leave the industry."

That tells me that the advisors are not just giving advice that is based simply on a conflict of interest. Many truly don't know what is in the best interest of their clients *or themselves.* When I was a broker, I was told to get out there and sell and pay little attention to the academic research being done in the world of investing.

My biggest concern with the fiduciary discussion is that it would cause investors to turn a blind eye toward their investments and say to themselves, "If my advisor has to do what is in my best interest, then I don't have to pay attention to what is going on." That is dangerous. I believe you need to understand your investments, because no one cares more about your money than you.

# End Notes

1. Bureau of Labor Statistics, *Occupational Employment and Wages,* U.S. Department of Labor, May 2016

2. Seeking Alpha Winners And Losers Among The First Batch Of Morningstar Analyst Ratings Apr. 13, 2017

3. For those of you who just have to know the Gordon Growth Formula flaws: One problem is that the formula assumes a constant growth rate, which is unrealistic. Another obvious flaw is regarding the dividend. If a company has no dividend, the formula would assign a value of zero—and many companies don't pay dividends.

4. Original sources from *The Wall Street Journal*

5. Campbell, John (Harvard University), Martin Lettau (New York University), Burton Malkiel (Princeton) and Yexiao Xu (University of Texas at Dallas), *"Have Individual Stocks Become More Volatile? An Empirical Exploration of Idiosyncratic Risk."* ©2000

6. All else is never really equal because expected earnings growth rates, risk, and other factors can vary widely between companies.

7. "More Perp Walks, Please." Jason Lahart, CNN.com, August 1, 2002

8. "Prison for Security Shapers" *The Literary Digest,* April 8, 1933

9. "Stop Lying to Investors," *Collier's Magazine:* July 29th, 1933

10. "The Challenge of Central Banking in a Democratic Society," Remarks by Chairman Alan Greenspan, At the Annual Dinner and Francis Boyer Lecture of The American Enterprise Institute for Public Policy Research, Washington, D.C., December 5, 1996

11. *NIV Bible,* Ecclesiastes 11:2

12. SPIVA® US Scorecard - Year-End 2016

13. Stossel, John (Broadcast) On-Air, ABC *20/20,* November 27, 1992.

14. "3 Important Lessons from the Downfall of Legendary Stockpicker Bill Miller" *Money Magazine:* August 17th 2016

15. "Most Investors Didn't Come Close Beating the S&P 500": *CNBC* Jan. 5th, 2017.

16. Dimensional Returns: 2017 - S&P 500/Russell 2000

17. CRSP 1-10, University at Chicago

18. "Investors Cloud the Crystal Ball," Bloomberg: Aug. 11th, 2017

19. SPIVA® US Scorecard, Year-end 2016

20. Morningstar® Advisor Workstation 2016 and Dimensional Returns 2016

21. "Stock Market Extremes and Portfolio Performance," A study commissioned by Towneley Capital Management and conducted by Professor H. Nejat Seyhun, University of Michigan

22. Yan, Xuemin Sterling, "The Determinants and Implications of Mutual Fund Cash Holdings: Theory and Evidence." *Financial Management,* Vol. 35, No. 2: Summer 2006

23. Michael C. Jensen, "The Performance Of Mutual Funds In The Period 1945-1964," Harvard Business School, *Journal of Finance:* Vol. 23, No. 2 (1967) 389- 416.

24. Charles D. Ellis, "The Loser's Game," *Financial Analysts Journal:* July-Aug 1975

25. Spread costs can vary based on time of day and volume and can be viewed on websites such as Yahoo Finance.

26. Deciphering Funds' Hidden Costs: *Wall Street Journal*, March 17th, 2004

27. Jason Karceski (University of Florida), Miles Livingston (University of Florida), and Edward O'Neal (Wake Forest University), "Mutual Fund Brokerage Commissions," January 2004.

28. "Mutual Fund Transaction Costs": Boston College, April 2015

29. Investment Company Institute, DFA Returns Software © 2017 Paul Winkler, Inc.

30. Gary P. Brinson, L. Randolph Hood, and Gilbert L. Beebower, "Determinants of Portfolio Performance," *The Financial Analysts Journal,* July/August 1986.

31. Graph used with the permission of Matrix Asset Allocation

32. Graph used with the permission of Matrix Asset Allocation

33. Based on the S&P 500

34. Morgan Stanley Europe, Australia, Far East Index; DFA returns software; The University of Chicago

35. Morningstar Direct, 2016

36. CRSP 9-10 Data, University of Chicago

37. Graph used with the permission of Matrix Asset Allocation

38. Graph used with the permission of Matrix Asset Allocation

39. DFA returns software and the University of Chicago CRSP database

40. M. Clayman, "In Search of Excellence: The Investor's Viewpoint." *Financial Analyst's Journal,* May-June 1987, pg. 63

41. Graph used with the permission of Matrix Asset Allocation

42. Returns chart used with the permission of Matrix Asset Allocation.

43. These portfolios assume that the funds used have the same returns as the underlying indexes. This is not possible since there are expenses connected to replicating the index. Actual results may be greater than or less than those illustrated.

44. William Bernstein, *The Four Pillars of Investing,* McGraw Hill: New York, 2002

45. "Post-fiduciary, 18% of advisers think about quitting" *Financial Planning Magazine* Sept. 26, 2016

# Answers to Chapter Quick Quizzes

## Chapter 1

### 1. Why do investors fail?

Humans tend to be driven by their emotions rather than by logic. Thus, when faced with financial decisions, logic and reason are often replaced by the fear that they will lose all their money. Thus, they react in ways that reflect that fear, and this often leads to bad financial decisions. The answer also lies in a perpetual cycle called the Investor's Dilemma that investors go through when it comes to making investment decisions.

### 2. What is The Investor's Dilemma?

The Investor's Dilemma is a seven-phase cycle that people go through that ultimately ends in frustration with the investing process, and it is the primary reason that investors fail.

### 3. What are the seven steps of the Investor's Dilemma?

1) Fear of the Future 2) Prediction of the Future 3) Past Performance 4) Information Overload 5) Emotion or Instinct-Based Decisions 6) Breaking the Rules 7) Performance Losses.

### 4. What is most investors' biggest underlying fear?

People are afraid they will run out of money before they run out of life.

5. **With age comes the realization that time is a <u>precious commodity.</u>**

6. **When investors are trying to determine where to invest their money, what is typically the first (and fatal) mistake they inherently make?**

   Most investors believe that they can determine what stocks or mutual funds will perform well by looking at past performance.

7. **Why does the investment industry put such an emphasis on past performance?**

   It boils down to pure marketing. Investment companies, firms, and portfolio managers know that using past performance figures will attract the majority of the new money being invested, so they use those numbers. Investors think past performance is helpful, so the industry will use that data to sell investments.

8. **What fact about humans do salespeople utilize as a sales tactic?**

   People buy on emotion and justify with logic.

9. **When we don't know what to do or who to believe—especially in light of how many claim to be "experts"—what or who are we easily influenced by?**

   We tend to lean on the opinions of a family member or an old family friend, or perhaps we are influenced by familiar investments.

10. **One common rule of investing is don't put all your eggs in one basket. What is the technical term for this phrase?**

   Diversification

11. **What is the most common outcome of engaging in market timing?**

   Time and time again studies show that investors who try to second-guess the market's direction will get burned.

12. **What two motivating factors drive investors to engage in unwise investment practices such as market timing?**

Some fund managers truly believe that they can beat the market. The other reason is a little less innocent—and it has to do with marketing. Since the majority of money flows to funds with the best short-term performance, a fund manager faces tremendous pressure to gamble with the portfolio. Since most investors are unaware that the success is random, the risk is worth taking if it results in money flowing toward the fund they are managing.

13. **How do we escape the Investor's Dilemma?**

The only lasting solution is education.

14. **Some say that knowledge is power; it's really <u>applied knowledge</u> that holds the key to your financial success.**

## Chapter 2

1. **All too often, what is the result when we jump into complex topics but lack an understanding of foundational principles?**

The result is that we tend to draw faulty conclusions and end up making grave mistakes that could cost us our financial futures.

2. **What is a common way that corporations raise capital?**

One way they raise money in this market is through the issuance of bonds.

3. **What is a bond?**

A bond is a tool that is used when a company, mortgagee, or governmental unit borrows money. Bonds are usually issued in even denominations of $1,000, $5,000 and $10,000, and they typically have a certain period of time before they mature.

4. **True or False: Many bondholders choose bonds because of their stability; and consequently, they are among the first groups in line to get their money back when the issuer of their bonds runs into financial difficulty.**

True

5. **What are the three maturity ranges associated with bonds?**

1) Short term—Less than five years 2) Intermediate—Between five and ten years 3) Long term—A maturity date over ten years.

6. **True or False: The shorter the amount of time a bond has until it matures, the greater the potential amount of volatility that can be experienced by the investor.**

False

7. **It is only one year from the date you made a five-year bond investment, but now you want to sell the bond. Interest rates have gone up in the market. What will you have to do to entice someone to buy it?**

You will have to drop the price. In other words, you must discount the bond so that the investor choosing between your bond and the new, four-year bond with a higher coupon rate will be indifferent between the two alternatives.

8. **Who is the lowest risk borrower?**

The Federal Government

9. **What is another phrase for inflation risk, and why is it called that?**

Inflation risk is often called the silent tax. We never see it, but it is always at work, destroying the purchasing power of our money.

10. **To help combat inflation, some bonds have inflation protection built into them. One example is "I-bonds." How do they work?**

They pay a certain level of interest every year on the principal. When inflation figures are announced, the principal value is adjusted to reflect the inflation number.

11. **What is one of the greatest benefits that bonds provide?**

Bonds can provide a powerful hedge against stock market downturns.

## Chapter 3

1. **What was the name of the document that created the first organized stock exchange in 1792?**

The Buttonwood Agreement

2. **What are the three major stock exchanges used today in the United States?**

The NYSE, the NASDAQ, and the NYSE American (formerly the American Stock Exchange).

3. **A <u>stock</u> is an instrument that shows that you are a part owner of a corporation.**

4. **If there is a company with 10,000 outstanding shares and you own 1,000 of those shares, how much of the company (in percentages) do you own?**

Ten percent

5. **Name one compelling reason to invest in stocks.**

Stocks are a great inflation hedge.

6. **The cost of goods and services are continually rising due largely to inflation.**

7. **True or False: The Gordon Growth Formula is useful for understanding many of the price movements we see in the stock market.**

   True

8. **What are capital markets?**

   The capital markets (also known as the stock and bond markets) are giant machines for raising money for companies who need it. Companies want access to your capital and they are willing to pay for the use of your money.

9. **What is the major difference between a bond payment and stock earnings?**

   You have a fighting chance that the stock's earnings will rise over time. The bond issuer has no obligation to pay you any more interest than they agreed to when they borrowed the money.

10. **What are the two primary types of risks when investing in stocks?**

    Non-systematic risk (also known as diversifiable risk) and systematic risk.

11. **A company's cost of capital is easy to determine with bonds. What must you look at to determine their cost of capital?**

    Look at the interest rates on borrowed money.

12. **True or False: If a company is selling at or near its book value, this is a sign that investors have confidence in the company.**

    False

# Chapter 4

**1. Sometimes knowledge isn't power. How can this be so?**

The harm is not in listening to the advice and examining its validity; rather, the harm lies in how we react to the information we receive.

**2. What does the old adage, "Sell in May and go away" mean? And is it true?**

The idea behind this phrase is to sell your stocks prior to the sleepy—and supposedly negative—summer months and return to the market again in the fall. No, the adage is not true. The problem is that the data used to prove this phrase was taken in isolation and had no logical, real-world basis. If a more thorough analysis had been done, commentators would have seen that markets actually move up more often than down during the summer months.

**3. What's often the best thing to do with the "doom and gloom" information from the media in regard to your investments?**

Ignore it.

**4. Why still invest if the economic outlook according to the media is so grim?**

The answer to that question can be answered by looking at an example from the Great Depression. Investors were discouraged from staying in the market, but all this did was drive them away just before the markets recovered. An investor pulling out of large U.S. stocks in April of 1933 missed out on well over 300 percent growth in their investments through August of 1937.

**5. What phrase did Alan Greenspan use in 1996 to describe what he saw as excess optimism on the part of investors and the media?**

Irrational exuberance

6. **Focusing on the top investments in previous years is analogous to playing the lottery with** <u>last week's</u> **winning numbers.**

7. **Why does the media continue to dispense advice that is not reliable or proven?**

It is because of marketing and the bottom line—keeping advertisers happy. They hype their info to sell more magazines and increase viewership.

# Chapter 5

1. **What is one of the oldest investing concepts known to mankind?**

It is the concept of diversification.

2. **Why do investors take on the risk of investing in small numbers of stocks and narrow segments of the market?**

It is largely due to a misunderstanding of the risk/return trade-off. Higher risk does not always equal a higher return, especially when those high risks are uncalculated or poorly executed.

3. **If we can't safely diversify on our own without having millions in capital, what choice do individual investors have?**

One solution is a commingled investment vehicle, which is an investment product that is the result of pooling multiple investors' assets.

4. **What are some common examples of commingled investment vehicles?**

Mutual funds, variable annuity sub-accounts, and exchange traded funds (ETFs).

5. **What is another term for unsystematic risk, and why is it called this?**

Uncompensated risk. It is uncompensated because—quite simply—there is no additional return expectation for the risk taken.

**6. What is the most common type of commingled investment?**

An open-end mutual fund

**7. What type of fee is charged upfront when buying a mutual fund, and what does this fee typically pay for?**

The fee is called a front-end load (or upfront charge). This upfront charge is used to compensate the broker and the brokerage firm that sold the fund.

**8. What are two potential problems with commission-based investing?**

1. Friction or expenses incurred when managing a portfolio due to front or back- end fund loads that may be payable.

2. Potential for conflicts of interest where the incentive is given to perform unnecessary trades, recommend higher commission funds or recommend products based on what is wanted versus what is needed.

**9. When it comes to mutual funds, it is often just a matter of <u>how</u> you will pay, not <u>if</u>.**

**10. However confusing it may seem, what is an important tool that should be used to choose investments for your financial future?**

A mutual fund prospectus

## Chapter 6

**1. What are the four basic categories of investing myths?**

1) The success of stock picking 2) Belief in market timing 3) Relying on past performance 4) The idea that costs don't matter.

**2. What is the only chance we have to escape the myths of investing?**

We must examine how they are used and why they don't work. In other words, "Know thy enemy."

**3. What is stock picking?**

It is the idea that an investor or an investment advisor utilizes their skill and knowledge to determine which stocks have the greatest promise of delivering good returns in the future.

**4. Who benefits from stock picking?**

Wall Street tends to benefit from our exaggerated belief in our stock picking aptitude far more than we, the individual investors, do.

**5. What has the fierce competition among mutual funds caused fund families to do?**

Because of the vast number of choices available, funds are desperate to stand out. Most fund families feel compelled to gamble with their investors' money in order to gain the spotlight. Fund managers feel tremendous pressure to find the stocks that will give them superior returns, and the result is that the average stock mutual fund turns its portfolio over at a rate of over 100 percent per year.

**6. What is typically true of actively managed funds?**

Actively managed funds cost investors part of their returns in almost every asset class or area of the stock market. No matter the area in which the fund manager is investing—small companies, large companies, international, etc—actual performance tends to lag that particular market segment.

**7. The financial media tends to keep the successful stock picking myth alive through their constant focus on <u>yesterday's winners</u>.**

8. **True or False: Stock prices are not directly related to shifts in supply and demand.**

   False

9. **Stock picking takes a process that should be based on realistic risk and reward and throws <u>logic, reason,</u> and <u>research</u> out the window.**

## Chapter 7

1. **What is market timing?**

   The act of market timing is any attempt to change the mix of your portfolio based on a prediction or forecast of the future.

2. **What assumption does the concept of market timing make?**

   It makes the assumption that entire segments of the market are mispriced.

3. **When an investor attempts market timing, it almost always results in what?**

   It results in lower returns than a buy-and-hold approach to investing.

4. **What are two specific types of market timing?**

   1) Tactical asset allocation 2) Style drift.

5. **Tactical asset allocation is a process where a mutual fund buys several different areas of the market and changes the emphasis based on their <u>market forecasts.</u>**

6. **What is the only difference between tactical asset allocation and the simpler form of timing between stocks and cash?**

   The difference is in the number of asset categories involved.

**7. What is one of the primary reasons that funds engage in style drift and other forms of market timing?**

One of the reasons funds engage in this activity has to due with fund marketing. If a fund can edge out its peers in short-term past performance, then they can gain a competitive advantage (in the short run, at least) in terms of positive press coverage and good ratings.

**8. Why doesn't market timing work?**

The stock market responds to new information far too quickly for investors to respond, and ultimately, for investors to benefit from that information. In addition, the costs to be out of the market when good news hits may be quite damaging. The underlying problem is that no one really knows when the best days will happen, and ultimately, this is what makes market timing so difficult.

**9. What are the signs to look for to determine whether your fund is engaging in market timing?**

Your fund may be engaging in market timing if the fund's mix between different areas of the market changes from year to year. Another sign that the fund is attempting to time the market is a large cash position in the fund.

## Chapter 8

**1. What is the most common disclaimer attached to investment products? Does it seem like investors believe it?**

Past performance is no guarantee of future results. No, from the actions of many investors, it seems that no one pays attention to this disclaimer.

**2. What is the primary purpose of magazine headlines promising to reveal the big winners?**

To entice us to buy the magazine so that we see the advertisements contained inside.

3. **True or False: Top performing managers who consistently perform for at least three years are statistically more reliable than those with only one year of successful returns.**

False

4. **According to Charles Ellis, investment managers are not beating the market; the market is <u>beating them</u>.**

5. **What is one of the biggest reasons why investment pros have such a difficult time matching simple market returns?**

It is because these professionals are so smart. They are an extremely competitive and intelligent group of people who, because of their level of intellect, tend to keep the market a level playing field. Sometimes they may get lucky and choose the right investment, and other times they'll be frustrated with a bad choice. In the end, however, it all evens out.

## Chapter 9

1. **What is the fourth myth of investing?**

The idea that expenses don't matter.

2. **What is the expense ratio or management fee?**

It is a fee that is assessed on the balance of your investment in the fund. The fee typically pays for costs associated with the management company, the fund distribution company, the custodian, the transfer agent, attorneys, and accountants.

3. **True or False: Because more effort is needed to fill orders (and therefore more risk is incurred), large companies tend to be more costly to trade.**

False

**4. Is it required that investment companies and fund managers provide detailed information on commissions on internal trades to investors? And why are companies reluctant to do so?**

No, it is not required. They are reluctant because it could put them at a competitive disadvantage. Publishing information that your competitors are not obligated to provide can cause problems.

**5. What is a soft dollar arrangement and how are soft dollars used?**

A soft dollar arrangement is where a mutual fund pays for research through the commissions they pay to a brokerage firm. Soft dollars represent a way for the manager to avoid paying for research out of the contracted fee with the fund and allow the manager to keep a greater portion of the fee as profit.

**6. If a mutual fund grows too large and is managing a great deal of client assets, any trading that the fund engages in can actually move stock prices against the fund. In other words, they will drive the price of stocks they are selling down and the price of stocks they are buying up. What is this phenomenon called?**

It is a concept called market impact.

**7. What is one of the best ways to avoid implicit and unnecessary fees and costs?**

Avoid funds that trade stocks too often.

**8. What is an effective way to determine which funds aren't engaging in excess trading?**

Look at the fund's turnover ratio, which can be found in the fund's prospectus. A turnover ratio of ninety percent means that ninety percent of the fund's assets were sold during the preceding year. The lower the ratio, the fewer number of trades were made that year.

9. **If you read in the prospectus that a fund manager's objective is to find underpriced stocks or to get rid of overvalued stocks, it's a sure sign that the fund will be subject to frequent trading.**

10. **A tax-managed fund may keep taxes low by engaging in any number of strategies including what?**

Low-turnover, off-setting capital gains with capital losses, holding stocks that historically keep taxable dividends low, selling higher basis stocks in order to avoid selling lower basis stocks, and rebalancing using cash flows

## Chapter 10

1. **What tool helps measure both upside and downside risk?**

Standard deviation

2. **What does standard deviation tell us in relation to a portfolio?**

Standard deviation is a measure that tells us how much our portfolio is likely to deviate or vary from the expected return.

3. **Things can always happen that have never occurred before. Standard deviation just gives us a tool to shed light on possible outcomes in the future based on the past.**

4. **The measurement of risk is a primary tool used in a process called probability analysis. What is another name for this process?**

Monte Carlo simulations

5. **True or False: The major problem that linear simulations solve is that returns in the market are unpredictable.**

False

**6. How does Monte Carlo simulation help determine the most efficient amount of money to contribute to your retirement fund?**

Through Monte Carlo simulation, you can determine if you should be saving more money or reducing the amount of your distribution in retirement by projecting different return scenarios and how you may be affected by each.

**7. What data is typically needed for a Monte Carlo calculation?**

Standard deviation of the portfolio, current accumulation, additional deposits anticipated, expected return, inflation rate expected, years to retirement, and amount of distribution in retirement.

**8. True or False: Monte Carlo simulation software is easy to use for beginning investors.**

False

## Chapter 11

**1. What are the primary causes of failure amongst investors?**

The lack of discipline and an absence of proper planning.

**2. What is the best way to feel confident enough to stay in your investments no matter the current economic climate?**

Make sure you know the why behind your portfolio design.

**3. The biggest problem in investing stems from not having any confidence in your own <u>investment strategies</u>.**

**4. True or False: Always remember that your choice to sell stocks is a prediction that the future will look like the immediate past.**

True

**5. What is the most important factor in portfolio performance?**

Asset allocation

**6. Name the six main asset classes.**

1) Treasury bills 2) Treasury bonds 3) Large U.S. stocks 4) Large international stocks 5) Small U.S. stocks 6) Small international stocks

**7. Which asset class has the lowest risk and what is its main purpose?**

Treasury bills. They protect the principal of our investments from short-term declines. This makes them useful for emergency funds and short-term goals. They are also useful in our portfolio as the one vehicle that will likely always go up.

**8. Because an investor is locking up money for a greater amount of time with T-bonds, they are prone to <u>interest rate</u> risk.**

**9. When it comes to stocks, in exchange for higher potential returns, what must investors contend with?**

Significantly higher volatility

**10. True or False: Because of their many similarities, large international stocks and large U.S. stocks always move in tandem with each other.**

False

**11. What are a few advantages of owning small U.S. stocks?**

They have provided even greater returns than large U.S. stocks throughout time. Small companies tend to move differently from large U.S. companies because they are typically more regional in focus. They can often implement new technology much faster than their large company counterparts. They often change direction faster as well, because there is commonly less bureaucracy. Small companies can serve to dampen volatility, because they don't usually move in lock step with other areas of the market.

**12. Despite the commonly held belief of the average investor that international stocks are too risky, what is true of small international stocks?**

Research in portfolio design actually shows that we can reduce risk by adding small international stocks to the asset allocation mix.

# Chapter 12

**1. What is the only lasting way to gain confidence in your investment decisions?**

Become educated and don't just trust what your investment advisor, family members, friends, or the media tells you. Make your own informed decisions that you can feel confident with.

**2. You can't build a lasting foundation in investment knowledge without knowing the <u>how</u> behind concepts and terminology.**

**3. What is the Efficient Frontier?**

It is a graph that represents portfolio mixes where the level of expected return is highest for a given level of risk that an investor is willing to take.

**4. The how behind the Efficient Frontier is based on what idea?**

That the different asset classes move in dissimilar fashion with one another. Therefore, putting them together in a portfolio causes the whole to be less risky than the parts.

**5. Typically, you should not rebalance your allocation unless your portfolio is deviating from your target percentages by <u>twenty-five</u> percent or more.**

**6. What does the Fama-French Three Factor Model help explain?**

The model explains that there are three factors responsible for approximately ninety-five percent of the levels of returns you can expect from a portfolio. By changing how much exposure you have to these factors, you can change the expected return of the portfolio, and this will also alter the amount of risk.

**7. What are the three factors considered in the Three Factor Model?**

1) Stocks vs. bonds 2) Small companies vs. large companies and 3) Value stocks vs. growth stocks.

**8. What is the first factor, stocks vs. bonds, often called? And what does it mean?**

The first factor is often referred to as the market factor. The market factor means that stocks are more risky than bonds with a larger percent standard deviation, but they also have higher return potential.

**9. Just as stocks tend to deliver higher returns over time, <u>small companies</u> tend to display higher returns than large companies.**

**10. The third factor of the Three Factor Model says that value stocks tend to outperform growth stocks over time. In layman's terms, what does this mean?**

This means that distressed companies tend to have higher returns than strong and stable companies. This is surprising because most of us believe that we should have nothing but great companies in our portfolios.

**11. It is important to remember that the market already does a pretty good job of making sure that pricing imperfections get eliminated; so big <u>bargains</u> aren't necessarily just sitting out there waiting for a better-informed investor to stumble upon them.**

**12. What commonly used ratio does the Fama-French model use to define value?**

Price to Book

**13. What tool can investors use to compare mutual funds and how does this tool work?**

The tool is the Morningstar Style Box, and it can be helpful as a starting point for choosing funds for your mix. The Morningstar Style Box attempts to classify mutual funds in nine different areas: Large growth, large blend, large value, mid- cap growth, mid-cap blend, mid-cap value, small growth, small blend, and small value.

## Chapter 13

**1. Choosing a portfolio mix often consists of picking mutual funds with the best track record. What is this method called and why is it called that?**

This selection method is the grocery store approach to investing, because it is very much like a shopper walking into the grocery store without a shopping list and just picking whatever looks or sounds good at the time.

**2. What is the first thing to determine before selecting your investments?**

You must first determine how long you have until you need your money back, or your time horizon.

**3. What are some other considerations in the investment selection process?**

Other considerations in the process may involve the amount of volatility you can stand and whether you are going to draw an income from the portfolio. Designing the right mix is a balancing act between the two different types of risk.

**4. What are the five different time horizons?**

1) One year or less 2) One to three years 3) Three to five years 4) Six to nine years 5) Ten plus years

**5. Historically, the stock market goes down one out of every <u>three</u> years.**

**6. Be careful when the interest rate appears to be "too good to be true." Why must you exercise caution in these cases?**

Some financial institutions have been known to take imprudent risks with investors' money just so they can advertise a high interest rate. The safest types of money market funds are backed by government debt for the reason we discussed—they can print money.

**7. If you are investing for one to three years, what percentage of that investment might go into stocks?**

You may choose to put up to twenty-five percent into stocks.

**8. If you have a goal that requires money four years from today, what should you do in relation to the percentage of stocks in your portfolio?**

You could slightly increase your holdings of stocks. Depending on your risk tolerance, this time horizon allows you to put up to fifty percent of your money in the stock market.

**9. What is the primary goal with an aggressive mix?**

The primary goal with this type of mix is to have maximum capital appreciation potential. This type of mix tends to give you the lowest long-term exposure to inflation risk.

**10. What particular part of your asset allocation is most often overlooked?**

International stocks

11. **I typically recommend looking at your portfolio at least <u>once a year</u> for rebalancing.**

12. **One method to determine what mix you should choose is to pick the right time horizon for you. What is another way to determine what type of allocation to choose?**

    Ask yourself how soon you will need to take an income from your investments.

13. **Diversified portfolios designed to provide an investor income should also contain a large portion of the money in bonds. Why?**

    Bonds don't move in lock step with stocks. If and when the general direction of stocks is down, the stock portion of the portfolio may go down more than the bonds go up, causing the total portfolio value to go down temporarily. It is during these times that you can take income from the bond segment of the portfolio.

14. **One of the most logical ways to take an income from your investments is to use the multiple wells approach. What does that mean?**

    Let's say there are ten different areas of the investment markets among which you've spread your money. You wouldn't expect each area to perform well every year. Since the goal of investing is to buy low and sell high, you should take your income from the area that is over-represented in your portfolio. It's like taking water from the highest well. In essence, the wells approach takes the emotion out of investing and allows stocks time to recover when markets are down.

## Chapter 14

1. **What is the most common reason why people change their portfolios?**

    The reason largely stems from the fact that they really don't have a proper set of expectations, and they likely do not know how their portfolios will respond during different types of markets.

**2. Although the phrase may apply to some areas of life, ignorance is <u>not bliss</u> when it comes to investing.**

**3. In the following formula, what do the letters stand for: (I + E) x M > C?**

Instincts plus Emotions magnified by the Media outweigh (are greater than) the Cognitive part of our minds.

**4. Who stands to gain the most by the fact that human beings make decisions based heavily on emotion and instinct?**

The ones who have the most to gain are those in the investment industry who can prey on our emotions to persuade us to act more frequently.

**5. What is the Macro Method?**

It is a way of judging your portfolio's performance by looking at whether your portfolio performed within expectations as a whole. You must look at the return over a calendar year and compare it to the range of returns you expected from the portfolio.

**6. How does the second method of portfolio performance, the Micro Method, differ from the Macro Method?**

With the Micro Method, you focus on the smaller picture or "parts" of your portfolio rather than the performance of the whole portfolio.

**7. True or False: Using evaluative methods such as the Macro and Micro Methods gives us a "permission slip" to just leave things alone and let market forces do their thing.**

True

**8. Confident investors are disciplined investors, and disciplined investors are far more likely to be <u>successful</u> investors.**